THE RED
ORCHESTRA

THE RED ORCHESTRA

Instruments of Soviet Policy
in Latin America
and the Caribbean

DENNIS L. BARK, editor

HOOVER INSTITUTION PRESS

Stanford University, Stanford, California

The Hoover Institution on War, Revolution and Peace, founded at Stanford University in 1919 by the late President Herbert Hoover, is an interdisciplinary research center for advanced study on domestic and international affairs in the twentieth century. The views expressed in its publications are entirely those of the authors and do not necessarily reflect the views of the staff, officers, or Board of Overseers of the Hoover Institution.

Hoover Press Publication 308

First printing, 1986
Manufactured in the United States of America
90 89 88 87 86   9 8 7 6 5 4 3 2 1
Library of Congress Cataloging in Publication Data
The Red orchestra.

   Includes bibliographies and index.
   1. Latin America—Foreign relations—Soviet Union—
Congresses.   2. Soviet Union—Foreign relations—
Latin America—Congresses.   3. Soviet Union—Foreign
relations—1953–1975—Congresses.   4. Soviet Union—
Foreign relations—1975-   —Congresses.
5. Communist strategy—Congresses.   6. Propaganda,
Communist—Latin America—Congresses.   I. Bark,
Dennis L.
F1416.S65R43   1986   327.4708   86-15181
ISBN 0-8179-8082-2 (alk. paper)

Design by P. Kelley Baker

Contents

Abbreviations

AAPSO	Afro-Asian People's Solidarity Organization
ABM	Antiballistic missile
ANC	African National Congress
ASW	Antisubmarine warfare
COWPE	Commission for Organizing the Party of the Working People of Ethiopia
CPSU	Communist Party of the Soviet Union
CRM	Revolutionary Coordination of the Masses (El Salvador)
DGI	Cuban Intelligence Service
DNU-MRH	National Unified Leadership of the Honduran Revolutionary Movement
DRU	Unified Revolutionary Directorate (El Salvador)
EGP	Guerrilla Army of the Poor (Guatemala)
EPRP	Ethiopian People's Revolutionary Party
ERP	People's Revolutionary Army (El Salvador)
ETA	Basque Fatherland and Freedom (Spain)
FAO	Large Opposition Front (Nicaragua)
FAR	Rebel Armed Forces (Guatemala)

FARN	Armed Forces of National Resistance (El Salvador)
FDR	Democratic Revolutionary Front (El Salvador)
FMLH	Marxist Front for the Liberation of Honduras
FMLN	Farabundo Marti National Liberation Front (El Salvador)
FPL	Farabundo Marti People's Liberation Forces (El Salvador)
FPL	Popular Liberation Forces (El Salvador)
FSLN	Sandinist National Liberation Front (Nicaragua)
GLCM	Ground-launched ballistic missile
GRU	Chief Intelligence Directorate (of the Soviet General Staff)
I.D.	International Department (of the CPSU)
ICBM	Intercontinental ballistic missile
IID	International Information Department (of the CPSU)
IMEiMO	Institute of World Economics and International Relations
IRA	Irish Republican Army
IRBM	Intermediate-range ballistic missile
KMT	Kuomintang (China)
MfS	Ministerium für Staatssicherheit (East German Ministry for State Security)
MIR	Movement of the Revolutionary Left (Chile)
MNR	National Revolutionary Movement (El Salvador)
MPL-Cinchoneros	Popular Liberation Movement (Honduras)
MPLA	Popular Movement for the Liberation of Angola
MRP-IXIM	People's Revolutionary Movement (Guatemala)
MVD	Ministry of Internal Affairs (Soviet Union)
NDP	New Democratic Party (Canada)
NJM	New Jewel Movement (Grenada)
OAU	Organization of African Unity
ORPA	Organization of the People in Arms (Guatemala)
PCES	Salvadoran Communist Party
PCH	Honduran Communist Party
PCI	Italian Communist Party

PDRY	People's Democratic Republic of Yemen (South Yemen)
PGT	Guatemalan Labor Party
PLO	Palestine Liberation Organization
PNP	People's National Party (Jamaica)
PRTC	Revolutionary Party of Central American Workers (Honduras and El Salvador, separate branches)
PSCh	Chilean Socialist Party
SALT	Strategic Arms Limitation Talks
SLBM	Submarine-launched ballistic missile
SSBN	Ballistic-missile-carrying submarine
SWAPO	South West Africa People's Organization
UNO	National Opposition Union (El Salvador)
URNG	National Revolutionary Unity of Guatemala
WPC	World Peace Council

Foreword

Dennis L. Bark

The purpose of this volume is to bring scholarly discipline and perspective to bear on analysis of a vital national security issue. This issue is Soviet use of proxy assets as an instrument of foreign policy. The subject has seldom been the beneficiary of research and analysis conducted at our nation's leading centers for advanced study. Given the significant role played by Soviet proxy assets in many parts of the world and the destabilizing effects this instrument of Soviet foreign policy has produced and is producing, this issue deserves—and, in fact, demands—much greater attention.

The USSR's utilization of proxy assets is of critical importance to the national security of the United States. Use of these assets affects the freedom and stability of every country where such assets have been mobilized or may be mobilized in the future, including Ethiopia, South Yemen, Egypt, Angola, Vietnam, Laos, Cambodia, Chile, Afghanistan, Portugal, Guatemala, Cuba, El Salvador, Grenada, and Nicaragua.

This volume is drawn from a conference sponsored by the Hoover Institution in Washington, D.C., in June 1984. The purpose of the conference was to examine, in general terms, the nature and orchestration of Soviet proxy assets. In this regard the first session focused on the following questions:

(1) How is the orchestration initiated, conducted, and monitored?

(2) How do the instruments used by the Soviet Union vary on a regional as well as a global basis?

(3) How does the array of Soviet political instruments affect public opinion in the United States and Western Europe?

(4) What is the USSR's modus operandi and what apparatuses are employed?

The specific aim of the second session was a direct consequence of the first. The conferees chose to look more closely at the operation of Soviet proxy assets in a particular region of the world. Because of the tremendous importance that the southern hemisphere of the Americas holds for the world as a whole and for the United States in particular, the case of Latin America and the Caribbean was selected for review.

The conference was planned as a forum for discussion, and initially it was not expected that the discussion would produce a published result. The aim was simply to bring together a group of experts on Latin America and the Soviet Union who shared a desire to analyze the orchestration of Soviet proxy assets. We anticipated, therefore, a discussion of various political, economic, and military elements as they relate to the USSR's use of proxy assets as an instrument of foreign policy. The points of view presented and their relation to one another made it abundantly clear, however, that the views and perspectives presented orally should be put on paper.

The editor and the contributors to this volume—who all participated in the conference—hope that their efforts will (1) shed light on a region of critical importance for the maintenance of peace, security, and freedom; (2) contribute to the analysis of a complex foreign policy area that demands rigorous investigation but has received very little serious and careful attention; and (3) emphasize the importance of this area with a view toward making it a legitimate and credible area of scholarly inquiry.

As the contributions to this volume clearly indicate, Soviet operations via proxies in the Third World are extensive and highly sophisticated. Very little is known about the phenomenon outside of government intelligence circles. Not only do we know comparatively little about it, but there is considerable reluctance to pursue scholarly research and analysis of the topic. Given the dramatic effects of the use of Soviet proxy assets in Latin America, Africa, and Southeast Asia, the United States and its allies would be well advised to devote significant resources and attention to analysis of this instrument of Soviet foreign policy.

This volume is divided in two parts. Part I provides a prospective and retrospective view of several aspects of Soviet foreign policy, introduces the concept of Soviet proxy assets, and discusses the apparatus. Part II focuses on three countries of Latin America and the Caribbean in which the use of this mechanism is especially well illustrated and is documented by compelling evidence. This volume should, therefore, illuminate an extremely complex subject and an issue of critical importance to national security.

Acknowledgments

This volume is the result of discussions among scholars who share a conviction that the subject of proxy assets as an instrument of Soviet foreign policy requires much more intensive analysis than it has received thus far at our nation's universities and centers for advanced study. The editor is, therefore, especially indebted to the contributors to this volume for the time they have taken to produce their respective essays from a largely informal context.

The assistance provided by the Hoover Institution Press and its excellent staff has been invaluable. Without their suggestions this volume would not have appeared in timely fashion.

The consistently wise and patient assistance of Janet Dutra of the Hoover Institution has been an instrumental part of this project since its beginning. She is accorded a special debt of appreciation that she will continue to merit as the project develops in the future.

Although not authors of essays, Harry Rowen, Paul Seabury, and Charles Wolf have contributed to this project in numerous ways. It is largely thanks to their interest and concern that this volume has been created. Responsibility for errors, omissions, or other sins, however, rests solely with the editor.

Contributors

Dennis L. Bark is a Senior Fellow of the Hoover Institution and directs its National Security Affairs Program. Dr. Bark serves as a Director of the United States Institute of Peace and is the editor of *To Promote Peace* (Hoover Institution Press, 1984). He is currently working on issues concerning relations between Western Europe and the United States.

Mark Falcoff is a Resident Fellow at the American Enterprise Institute for Public Policy Research in Washington, D.C. Dr. Falcoff has been the recipient of a National Fellowship at the Hoover Institution and has authored *Small Countries, Large Issues* (1984).

Francis Fukuyama is a Senior Staff Member in the political science department of the Rand Corporation. He has also served on the Policy Planning Staff of the Department of State and is a specialist in Soviet–Third World affairs.

H. Joachim Maitre is Professor of Journalism and Professor of International Relations at Boston University, specializing in defense studies. He is also foreign affairs' editor of the quarterly *Strategic Review* (Washington, D.C.).

Uri Ra'anan is Professor of International Politics and Director of the International Security Studies Program at the Fletcher School of Law and Diplomacy, and a Fellow of the Russian Research Center at Harvard. He is the author of numerous publications, including works on the U.S.-Soviet strategic balance and on Soviet foreign policy.

Michael S. Radu is a Research Associate with the Foreign Policy Research Institute in Philadelphia, and a Peace Fellow with the Hoover Institution (1984–85). His writings include works on revolutionary regimes and movements in Latin America and sub-Saharan Africa.

Herbert Romerstein is Special Assistant to the Associate Director for Programs of the United States Information Agency. He is the coauthor (with Dr. Michael Ledeen) of *Grenada Documents: An Overview and Selection*), published in 1985 by the Department of State and Department of Defense. The views expressed in this volume by Mr. Romerstein are his own and do not necessarily reflect the view of the United States government.

Henry S. Rowen is Professor of Public Management at the Graduate School of Business and Senior Research Fellow of the Hoover Institution at Stanford University. He is former Chairman of the National Intelligence Council, President of the Rand Corporation, Assistant Director of the Bureau of the Budget, and Deputy Assistant Secretary of Defense.

Paul Seabury is Professor of Political Science at the University of California at Berkeley and served as a member of President Reagan's Foreign Intelligence Advisory Board from 1982 to 1985. Dr. Seabury writes on problems of American foreign policy. He is coeditor, with Walter A. McDougall, of *The Grenada Papers* (1984).

Richard H. Shultz, Jr. is Associate Professor of International Politics at the Fletcher School of Law and Diplomacy and serves as consultant to various U.S. government agencies concerned with national security affairs. He is coauthor, with Roy Godson, of *Dezinformatsia: Active Measures in Soviet Strategy* (1984).

Charles Wolf, Jr. is Director of the International Economic Policy Program of the Rand Corporation and Dean of the Rand Graduate School, as well as a Senior Research Fellow of the Hoover Institution. Dr. Wolf's current work focuses on the economic costs of the Soviet empire and on strategies for dealing with Soviet-sponsored political and military activities abroad.

THE RED
ORCHESTRA

Introduction

Dennis L. Bark, Henry S. Rowen, Paul Seabury, and Charles Wolf, Jr.

This introduction is meant to be more than a preliminary sketch of the basic ideas examined in this book. Its intent is to present a broad and important problem, namely, the design, purpose, and operational procedures of "The Red Orchestra."[1] In the body of the book that problem will be illustrated by specific reference to the case of Latin America and the Caribbean.

The use of proxy forces to engage an enemy is surely as old as the history of war among organized states. Communist parties, however, are unusual in having expanded the employment of such forces to an extent never before witnessed. The question before us is whether the manner in which the Red Orchestra operates, particularly in regions such as Latin America and the Caribbean, is crucial to the defense of the West.

For some time Western analysts have been observing novel patterns in the Soviet use of instruments of influence abroad. Although the USSR's deployment of such forces in dealing with its enemies is not new, it is important to recognize that the Soviet state was the first great power in history to field such forces on a global scale. By the 1930s, the Comintern, its front organizations, Communist trade unions, and local Communist parties operated in most regions of the world in various combinations. After World War II, these organizations were also augmented by forces of the Red Army and adjacent satellite ground forces, both in Europe and Asia.

By the 1970s, the means of influence manifest in widely separated regions of the world had become far more complex and ambitious than the traditional communist techniques. As R. Bruce McColm of Freedom House recently put it:

"All this makes the days of the Abraham Lincoln Brigade and the 1930's Front groups look like the Stone Age." The new developments also raise questions about the significance of this particular form of "diplomacy" for Western independence. The procedure is original and effective in widening Soviet influence. It is low in cost and low in risk, with a high potential for success. It is also a good deal more than that—it may pose a serious threat to world peace.

A novel ingredient in the Soviet approach is a capacity simultaneously to orchestrate and focus diverse elements of influence on many targets in different regions. Of particular interest is the synchronized participation of the forces of many communist states and movements in efforts to attain geographically distant and disparate targets. These forces, in alliance with supportive noncommunist states (such as the Libya of Moammar Khadafy) and movements (such as the Palestinian Liberation Organization of Yassir Arafat), today pose a grave threat to the West, the full dimensions of which are poorly understood.

These combinations have appeared at a time when the Soviet Union's own independent capacity to project military, air, and naval-maritime power has also taken on global dimensions. The two phenomena are intimately related and mutually reinforcing.[2] Since the geographic theaters in which such combined operations are far apart and have marked cultural and political differences, Western observers have thus far found assessment of their total weight and significance very difficult.

One impediment to our understanding of those Soviet operations lies in the fact that Western analysts of particular Soviet regional proxy operations normally are ill-informed as to the nature of similar operations elsewhere or of possible interregional strategic and functional connections. An Africanist familiar with Soviet operations in Libya, Angola, Mozambique, Namibia, Ethiopia, and southern Africa hardly can be expected to be familiar with analogous operations in Latin America or Asia. Moreover, regional political cultures and their attendant problems, which may arise sui generis, naturally impede comprehension of the totality or of the interrelationship of the parts.

To dwell upon the particular and the familiar encourages the parochial view that local problems first give rise to intervention or invite external influence. In this view, external influence and intervention are responses to an opportunity to discover, to identify, and to exploit genuine, pre-existing, and inevitable local conflicts.

There is much in this view. Indigenous and widely pervasive conditions of hardship, poverty, and inequality provide fertile grounds in which hostility, resentment, and instability flourish. Moreover, it is evident that the wealthy, industrialized parts of the world—at least recently, and certainly since the 1950s—have been politically much more stable than the poor regions. But such a view ignores the fact that Soviet subversive activities are also present (they have long been applied against and within industrialized democracies as well).

Revolution may have various immediate causes, including some that are Soviet-inspired, as well as some that are not. However, the consolidation of Leninist regimes in various parts of the world has, as a necessary condition, deliberate and coordinated action by Moscow. In practice, this means that internal causes serve as the vehicles and, sometimes, as the rationalization for the application of external influence and intervention by the Soviet Union. Such intervention is also designed to prevent reversion to a non-Leninist condition. The Soviet record in this regard is impressive. Without Soviet influence there would be some degree of turmoil in the world; with Soviet influence and intervention the degree is enormously increased.

There are nine principal instruments of influence employed by the Soviet government:

1. Conventional Soviet diplomatic activity, including the use of Soviet diplomatic personnel for overt and covert objectives.

2. Coordinated political action carried out by, for example, Communist parties, front organizations, and covert political operations.

3. Propaganda activities employing all forms of the media; again, covert media activities are important.

4. Intelligence gathering, analysis, dissemination, and operations; counterintelligence activities including active measures designed to manipulate and to deceive.

5. Provision of internal security services for local regimes, together with military and nonmilitary advisers and experts.

6. The transfer of arms and related supplies and maintenance capability.

7. The transfer of resources in the form of goods in kind (for example, oil), as well as cash and credit.

8. External combat forces from non-Soviet sources (such as Cuba, North Korea, Vietnam, or Libya), and, less frequently, from the Soviet Union itself.

9. Overt and covert support of terrorist groups and activities.

The admixture of instruments used in particular cases varies widely. It seems to be determined by local needs and constraints, attentiveness to possible reactions, and countermoves by adversaries. It may also be affected by budgetary limitations, Moscow's caution in avoiding situations that might escalate dangerously, opposition by some members of the Soviet bloc to participation in particular ventures, and so on.

The chief obstacle to our understanding of the current array of Soviet assets is superficial in nature. It is said to lie, on the one hand, in the sparse documentation of even the more visible activities of this system, and, on the other hand, in the dearth of knowledge as to how Soviet central authorities, and others, organize these disparate and far-reaching activities. A closer look, however, reveals that much publicly available information exists in the form of analysis prepared by observers of separate activities. The problem is that the information is fragmentary and diffuse and has not been gathered together in any organized and systematic fashion. The data have not been given a structure and are not available to the public in a coherent way.

At present, one can easily locate and identify such coordinating agencies as, for example, the International Department of the Soviet Central Committee. One also can speculate as to their roles, although without a sufficient body of knowledge as to how actual operations are conducted, what modes of orchestration are employed, or how primary responsibilities are managed. At this stage, therefore, we need to engage mainly in a synthetic reconstitution of the Soviet system by examining its activities around the world as they emerge in operation. We need to provide the foundation for the creation of a body of essential knowledge and for the balanced analysis of what our information means.[3]

In the nineteenth-century origins of Gestalt psychology we find a parallel to the intellectual difficulties faced here. Gestalt psychology began as protest against piecemeal analysis of atomistic experience. Its primary tenet was that even a brilliant investigation of parts cannot lead to an understanding of the whole. To understand the nature of the whole, analysis must also proceed "from above, down." An *understanding of the structure of the whole then leads to an understanding of the relationship of the parts to each other, of the total relationship among them, and finally of the collective relationship to the whole*; since the whole has a nature transcending the interweaving of the parts. Therefore, what is the whole? Certainly it must be more than the sum of its parts.

In the 1970s, it was first seen that Soviet expansion into the regions of northern, western, eastern, and southern Africa involved the deployment not only of Soviet assets—arms, troops, military and political advisers, secret police, and economic aid—but also those of other Soviet-bloc countries. Functional specialization evolved among the several interveners. In eastern and western Africa and in Namibia (as well as in Libya and in Yemen), East German police authorities supplied technical skills in the construction and control of internal security forces, concentration camps, and so forth. Bulgaria has played the leading role in the unsuccessful attempt to destabilize Turkey. In Africa, Cuban troops typically were at the forefront (albeit not exclusively) of the fighting against anticommunist resistance forces.

In the 1980s, from what has been learned in Central America and the Caribbean, this network has attained increased complexity and density. In the instance of the consolidation of Soviet power on tiny Grenada, U.S.-captured documents show direct human and material involvement not only of the Soviets and Cubans, but also of the Nicaraguan Sandinistas, Vietnam, Czechoslovakia, Bulgaria, East Germany, North Korea, Libya, Syria, Iraq, and the ubiquitous PLO—not to mention support groups drawn from the communist proxies and from other leftist organizations in the United States and Britain, as well as from within the Socialist International. Thus, when Grenada was freed from the New Jewel Movement in 1983, Westerners for the first time could observe not only the inner workings of a Marxist-Leninist regime but also the incredible impact of a large assemblage of Soviet proxies focused on a tiny island (see Paul Seabury and Walter A. McDougall, eds., *The Grenada Papers* [San Francisco: Institute for Contemporary Studies, 1984]).

In the spirit of Gestalt psychologists, we, the four cochairmen of this study of Soviet proxies, believe that one way to gain a fuller understanding of this problem would be, initially, to identify and bring together scholars and analysts of this subject who have dealt with it professionally from the following separate perspectives:

1. *Regional* perspectives of key geographic and cultural/political areas and key nations.

2. *Central* perspectives provided by Soviet experts in Kremlinology.

3. *Functional* perspectives on strategies of the Soviets and their clients in their international and transnational institutions and movements, including those not now under Soviet control.

4. *Historical* perspectives derived from Marxist-Leninist strategies.

The initial stage of this investigation is the gathering of data on the activities of actors among the networks—the who, what, and how of our problem. Our assumption is that we should not frame a Procrustean matrix within which to fit our evidence, but rather we should encourage the evidence to reveal the contours of the form even though it is as yet insufficient to allow us to understand the inner dynamics.

In the course of such a preliminary observation of the parts, we cannot fail to gain insight into matters of great importance. If our preliminary purpose is to learn how these Soviet proxy systems operate severally and in conjunction with each other, our ultimate object is to shed light on their chief inmost principles. These can hardly be confined to the operational sphere. But a better empirical understanding of the complex relationships among and between the parts can allow for a better comprehension of the whole.

To move in that direction, the following questions require answers:

1. What and where are the chief coordination centers of Marxist-Leninist groups and parties for specific activities? (as, for example, the International Department of the Central Committee of the Communist Party of the Soviet Union). How is the division of labor among countries determined and orchestrated?

2. When and to what extent do the Soviets, in diverse regions, micromanage activities abroad? Where and to what extent is such micromanagement turned over to other communist states and movements? (The inner diplomacy of the communist world—the continual comings and going of key party, government, and military leaders and delegates—can easily be mapped from public sources.)

3. Where and to what extent can it be discerned that operations are, on balance, locally inspired, initiated, and carried out? (For example, there is evidence that Castro has proposed initiatives that have then been approved and joined by Moscow.)

4. Given certain conditions indigenous to the Third World[4] (poverty, inequality, or political instability; that is to say, valid, authentic, unresolved grievances), to what extent do local seekers of power, or shaky holders of it, seek support of the Red Orchestra? And, on the contrary, to what extent does the activity of the Red Orchestra impress itself on and guide the evolution of local events? To what extent, and why, are local groups subsidized by other (non-Soviet) Marxist-Leninist, or radical anti-Western, regimes?

5. What are we to make of the probability that in some operational theaters the initiative and direction may arise from and pass through multiple centers? If so, then what sorts of frictions arise among them? How are such frictions resolved or exacerbated?

6. What in general and in particular can be discovered concerning the "political economy" of these very different enterprises? (As there is no free lunch, so there can be no free subversion.) What do they cost? Who pays? To what extent, for example, are proxy contributions to overseas activities a quid pro quo? Or are the funds gladly donated, being deemed beneficial both to a larger revolutionary cause and to the specific interests of the state concerned?[5]

7. To what extent are operations well beyond areas bordering the Soviet Union, over which Moscow is strategically weak, primarily intended to divert and distract American energies and to sow dissension in the Western camp?

8. What are the weaknesses and vulnerabilities of the Red Orchestra? It has had failures; what can be learned from them?

As we begin to seek answers to the questions raised thus far and speculate about their significance, we ought to recall that the questions, as well as the answers, are not independent of one another. In tracing and mapping the many interconnections of these proxy support operations, an initial task could be to define and set forth the separate yet reinforcing networks.[6]

It cannot be overemphasized that the attainment of such an overview—cartographic and analytical—would benefit not only perplexed specialists but, in simplified form, the public at large. Public attention to communist subversion invariably fixes on particularities rather than patterns; its perception is sequential rather than temporally holistic; it is constantly diverted from one venue to another when enlivened by the shock of new events. Both patterns and tendencies thus go unrecognized.

At this early stage of our inquiry into the operational modes of the Red Orchestra, we might, nevertheless, venture several generalizations about the whole, though acknowledging that they might have to be modified or even discarded in the light of subsequent evidence:

□ The conduct of political-paramilitary war by the Soviet Union, acting in concert with its partners, appears to be constrained mainly by the fluctuating appearance of opportunities for these orchestrated operations. The relative absence of constraints on the "supply side" of these operations may be due to either or both of two explanations: the high priority accorded these activities in the allocation of Soviet resources and efforts and/or the existence of excess capacity within the Soviet Union and among its allies for exploiting such opportunities when they arise.

It is also true that the Soviet Union does not take advantage of every opportunity that presents itself. But the Soviet government does stand committed by its very constitution to the support of so-called wars of national liberation, and Soviet theorists have developed a doctrine of "proletarian internationalism" to justify external intervention in support of "progressive forces" all over the world. One should ask, therefore, whether a lack of excess capacity in the Soviet Union led to a mandate placed on terrorist organizations, in particular, to finance their activities themselves rather than relying on the Soviet government for financial support, as in the past. What positive incentives drive the proxies to invest their own assets in these undertakings? What happens to such movements if and when the Soviets substantially reduce or cut off support? What indigenous sources of funding are available to them (for example, the drug traffic)?

□ In decisions about where and when to develop and expand these operations, particularly in the Third World, it appears that there is a substantial delegation of responsibility and initiative by the Soviet Union to its partners. Thus, for example, in the Caribbean region a considerable degree of initiative and responsibility evidently rests with Cuba as the concertmaster within the Red Orchestra. It appears, however, that, though such delegation exists, the orchestra leader—the Soviet Union— pays most of the bills.

☐ Although the precise location of decisionmaking with respect to these activities is obscure, there are some reasons for thinking that coordination in the use of various instruments is focused in the International Department of the Central Committee of the Communist Party of the Soviet Union; within the Cuban structure the focus lies in the American Department.

☐ The standard operating procedures of these activities entails the acquisition or enhancement of legitimacy for so-called wars of national liberation by using a network of sympathetic groups in the United States and in Western Europe. (For example, in El Salvador, a sophisticated computer-based filing system developed and used by the Salvadoran guerrilla "liberators" had been originally based on information provided from sources within the United States.)

☐ The cost of such activities expanded substantially after 1970. Soviet support for Cuba, Vietnam, and other countries expanded, and, in general, Soviet activities in politically less stable regions increased.

There remains an elusive and yet crucial matter that warrants several preliminary thoughts: namely, the spirit that animates this new and complex global phenomenon. It is all too easy for complacent Americans to dismiss, or to belittle, the importance of the sources and quality of enthusiasm in significant undertakings. This applies, in particular, to our understanding of the current relationship of Marxist-Leninist ideology to action in the communist world and elsewhere.

This matter has been a subject of new interest among philosophers and intellectuals in Europe and also among important American statesmen and opinion makers. Some of these people announce or prophesy the death of Marxist-Leninist doctrine and thought as inspiration to action, to obedience, and to an understanding of the world. For some, the appeals of communism are evidently long dead. This may well be true of most East Europeans, notably, at the present time, the Poles. The recent waning of communist ideology among West German youth has been matched, in France, by its rapid demise among most French intellectuals. For them, Marxism-Leninism may be irrelevant either as belief system or as guide to action. Descriptions of the nomenklatura system in the Soviet Union support the assertion that there are few true Marxists there (but many Leninists).

An asserted collapse of ideology may mean, however, that so-called ideological movements are becoming, by design, increasingly pragmatic, and that the waning of ideological fervor may actually result in the rise of revolution for its own sake. One thing is certain: the patterns of action in different regions are not always the same. The time frames also vary in length. Moreover, different activities conducted in different countries and parts of the world may represent very significant pieces of a puzzle consisting of widely disparate parts, seemingly unconnected—such as propaganda efforts, combined arms operations, and attacks on the stability of traditional institutions including the church, labor unions, universities, and respected political parties.

This question of ideological decline should be critically examined. In the Grenada documents, for instance, a reader is forcefully struck both by the fidelity shown by members of the New Jewel Movement to Leninist doctrines and by the intense convictions and enthusiasms that the doctrines evidently inspired. The appeals of communism here were clearly authentic; it also appears that this is the case in Latin America. In trying to understand these proxy states and movements, there is a need to typologize accurately their several organizational orientations. There also is a need to understand the diverse nuances of the convictions and beliefs that first give rise to political action and to feelings of international solidarity. Finally, there is a need to define the issues clearly—not to leave such definitions to a Soviet monopoly.

With respect to belief, we again must ask whether we have here a dynamic whole, the parts of which are not merely extended arms of Soviet ideology per se but possess among themselves a reinforcing collective vitality, enthusiasm, and solidarity. In this regard, the leftist affinities and solidarities of Third World movements and movement-states find a certain parallel in developments within the worldwide Roman Catholic Church. In this case, liberation theology (preoccupied with the secular and mundane) challenges the redeeming and transcendental missions of the church. The choices and dilemmas faced by the Vatican in the face of "revolutionary dynamic spontaneity" may not be dissimilar to those currently faced by the Soviets in their dealings with far-flung, Leninist movements of diverse natures.

Moscow, indeed and to be sure, asserts a standing claim to be the center of world Marxism-Leninism. But, to the extent that solidarities and affinities exist in Third World countries, they derive their spirit from a multitude of sources, in addition to the wellspring of Marxism-Leninism in the Kremlin. The admixture of anti-Americanism, anticapitalism, xenophobic nationalism, Leninism, and leftist renderings of global trends (on behalf of "the cause of all oppressed and exploited peoples") can be spontaneously enriched by intellectuals, journalists, scholars, or self-proclaimed representatives of the people, without direct, continuous guidance from a center. At the same time, the admixture can also be very easily enriched by direct, as well as indirect, guidance or attention in any number of different forms. It is safe to conclude that freedom and individual liberty are directly contrary to the tenets of Marxism-Leninism; but it should also be unequivocally clear that antipathy for the individual rights of man, on behalf of despots and totalitarian governments, long predates the Bolshevik revolution.[7]

Yet, despite diverse sources of animosity, the common denominator for most of these proxy states and movements, together with their Soviet sponsor, now appears to be the linkage of old-fashioned power seeking with the idea of a vanguard party implementing the dictatorship of the proletariat, which in turn is connected to the idea of proletarian internationalism.

Those who express the view that the appeal of Marxist-Leninist ideology has waned or disappeared are at least premature. It is true that the dismal economic performance and loss of liberties of this system in the Soviet empire and in China have eroded its attraction in the West, in Eastern Europe, and, apparently, in the Soviet Union itself. Deng Tsao Peng's extraordinary economic liberalizing reforms in China in the past few years are perhaps the most dramatic acknowledgment of this trend. It could be a mistake, however, to think that the appeal of Marxist-Leninist ideology is determined solely by its promise for generating economic performance or advancing human freedom. Another and sometimes dominant facet of its attraction is its utility as a guide and instrument in the acquisition, concentration, expansion, and preservation of political and military power by indigenous elites, especially today in poor countries. Experience in this dimension of performance has been very substantial, and the appeal this exercises in poor countries seems largely unimpaired by the system's failures.

This volume, as set forth in the foreword, represents a step in the consideration of Soviet proxy assets and their significance. The importance ascribed to such assets has been likened to instruments of an orchestra by members of the Soviet government. It was thus deemed appropriate to entitle this volume *The Red Orchestra*. What this means, in terms of the conduct of Soviet foreign policy, has been expressed most clearly by the former head of the Soviet government:

> The battle of ideas in the international arena is going on without respite. We will continue to wage it vigorously . . . our entire system of ideological work should operate as a well-arranged orchestra in which every instrument has a distinctive voice and leads its theme, while harmony is achieved by skillful conducting.[8]

NOTES

1. "The Red Orchestra" is the English translation of "Die Rote Kapelle," the Soviet underground apparatus active in Germany and Switzerland during World War II.

2. Soviet airlift capabilities since 1975, for example, have made it possible to ferry and resupply Cuban troops from the Caribbean to Africa and the Middle East.

3. There is an adage that the only Kremlinologists are those who live in the Kremlin. This is, however, not necessarily true; for, very often, one does not see until one seeks. In other words, one does not find something until one looks for it. See, for example, Robert W. Kitrinos, "International Department of the CPSU," *Problems of Communism* 33 (September–October 1984): 47–75.

4. We use this term to refer to poor and politically less stable countries, which are more vulnerable, therefore, to asserted "revolutionary" forces.

5. In the case of Central America and the Caribbean, one plausible if partial explanation for the contributions of such disparate donors as Libya, Vietnam, North Korea, and East Germany is that massive trouble for the United States in these regions might ultimately lead to a hemispheric retraction of U.S. power to the North American continent. These states thus would be collateral beneficiaries of an overall Soviet grand strategy.

6. In this regard, a model could take the form of those encyclopedic maps that have several transparent overlays. The orchestration of various forces at given times then could be compared and better understood, region by region. (One such transparency, for instance, could depict the diverse sources and way-stations of support in Central America and the Caribbean, and the specific natures of donated assistance on this one transparency could be depicted in different flowchart colors.) This is, perhaps, an appropriate future undertaking.

7. The emergence of Ayatollah Khomeini's Iran as a supporter of the Sandinistas illustrates the point that not all forces hostile to democracy and to the United States are aligned politically with Moscow.

8. Konstantin Chernenko, in an address to the Central Committee of the Communist Party of the Soviet Union, June 14–15, 1983, as cited in *Information Bulletin* (Prague), 16/1983.

PART I

Retrospective and Prospective

Uri Ra'anan

No less a document than the (current) "Brezhnev" Constitution of the USSR contains specific reference to Soviet activities in the Third World as a fundamental component of Soviet international policy. (The earlier "Stalin" Constitution did not deal with this matter at all.) Article 28 of the text states, "The foreign policy of the USSR is directed at . . . supporting the struggle of peoples for national liberation and social progress, at preventing aggressive wars." It must be remembered that, in other basic Soviet documents, "aggressive wars" are defined by their *class* content, ignoring such issues as who initiated the conflict or who is attempting to upset the existing balance. All wars, according to this definition, are just, as far as the role of members of the Soviet bloc and their Third World clients is concerned, whereas all attempts by the other side to resist are unjust. Whether a struggle should or should not be deemed supportive of "national liberation and social progress" is decided subjectively, that is, by the Soviet leadership itself. Consequently, in instances in which East and West have changed partners in the Third World, yesterday's "struggle . . . for national liberation" has become today's "aggressive war," or vice versa. This enables the Soviet leadership to pursue its inroads into the Third World with a great deal of tactical flexibility.

Portions of this chapter reflect material contributed by the author to a Special Report of the Institute for Foreign Policy Analysis, in 1985, under the title *Vulnerabilities of Third World Marxist-Leninist Régimes: Implications for U.S. Policy*. The author wishes to express his gratitude to the Institute for its permission to use this material.

The very concept of utilizing surrogate actors is based, of course, precisely on such flexibility. Although the practice is as old as history itself and certainly dates back, in the Soviet case, to the earliest days of the regime (to mention only the exploitation of the Comintern network by Lenin and Stalin), its contemporary phase may be traced back, paradoxically enough, to a U.S.-USSR understanding, during what were regarded as the halcyon days of so-called détente. The June 22, 1973, *Agreement Between the United States of America and the Union of Soviet Socialist Republics on the Prevention of Nuclear War* states, in part, that "The parties [the two signatory states] agree . . . that each party will refrain from the threat or use of force against . . . the allies of the other party and against other countries in circumstances which may endanger international peace and security." This codified the "Basic Principles" that the two superpowers, acting on behalf of the two opposing blocs, had endorsed on May 29, 1972, during the Moscow Summit (which was crowned by SALT I and the ABM treaty). These principles committed the parties to refrain from exploiting crisis situations, particularly in the Third World, for unilateral gains and from initiating action there without giving prior notice to the other side.

Presumably, the Soviet Union embarked on the détente process believing that it had something to gain from agreements on such topics as SALT. Certainly, one way of jeopardizing that process was through overt and blatant violation of the June 22 agreement. Not only would such encroachment strengthen the influence of those in the West who already harbored deep suspicions of Soviet intentions, but it was bound to deprive the Western arms-control lobby of its political ammunition. After all, it would be hard to present the Soviet Union as negotiating in good faith on arms control if it were simultaneously violating two protocols governing the general behavior of both the superpowers.[1]

The terminology of these agreements allowed the Soviet leadership to circumvent the spirit without violating the letter of the understanding. For several years following 1972–1973, the USSR established a military presence in precisely the areas that had been the object of the agreements, resorting to military and security elements of communist countries that were *not* members of the Warsaw Pact—Cuba, Vietnam, and North Korea—and thus could be viewed as outside the parameters of the texts in question.

A major consideration, evidently, was that the use of these particular proxies could serve, if not directly to "disinform" opponents, at least to provide the West with the means by which to deceive itself. Thus, from 1975 onward, a Vietnam-weary United States was presented with an incursion into Angola by elements from a Caribbean island state with a population of less than 10 million. Had the USSR adopted an overt combat role, instead of confining itself more discreetly to logistical tasks, could the Clark Amendment have been passed or could an American diplomat have remained in office after describing the Soviet Union as "a stabilizing force in Africa"? From the Western point of view, is the potential impact on vital sea lines of communication less significant because Cubans were involved rather than the Red Army? When the USSR utilized Cubans to achieve Soviet goals, not only did Moscow pay no price for such ventures, but Fidel Castro did not forfeit his role among the nonaligned and garnered plaudits from the U.S. ambassador to the United Nations.[2]

The tepid Western reaction to the initial phase of proxy warfare encouraged the Soviet leadership to escalate to a new level by introducing Warsaw Pact elements. Perhaps the consideration was that Cuban efficiency left something to be desired, even if Castro's men blended in better with their surroundings than blond East Germans. It seems fair to speculate that the relative apathy with which this step was received, less than half a decade after the 1972–1973 agreements, persuaded Moscow that it could move one step further and introduce the Red Army itself—in Afghanistan. (To be sure, Soviet combat units had appeared prior to 1972, particularly in Egypt, and had flown combat missions over the Suez Canal, but they were withdrawn in 1972.)

In the same context, there has been constant escalation also in another form of Soviet involvement that is not very far removed from proxy warfare, namely, the transfer of weapons. This can be evaluated not merely in absolute terms, to the extent that the upgrading of hardware everywhere has been reflected also in Soviet arms supplies to developing countries, but, more significantly, when measured relatively against the level of sophistication of matériel deployed on the Warsaw Pact–NATO central front. Thus, the weapons transferred to recipient countries in the mid-1950s predominantly consisted of World War II hardware that the Red Army and its allies were beginning to phase out as obsolete. By the end of that decade, the types of arms shipped to the Middle East and elsewhere were still in use in Warsaw Pact countries, although obsolescent and due to be replaced in the not too distant future. In the 1960s, the hardware in question was still in full use in the bloc, even though some more modern prototypes had made their appearance. By the 1970s and, especially, in the last five years, the USSR has been providing such countries as Syria, Libya, Iraq, and India with items that, in many instances, have not yet been received by Moscow's allies in the Warsaw Pact and that the Soviet Union itself has only just deployed. The result is that, qualitatively, and, in the case of the Middle East, even quantitatively, such Third World conflict arenas now hardly lag behind the European central theater itself (except for nuclear weapons, of course).

Although, as far as individual Third World countries are concerned, the USSR may well be focusing simply on targets of opportunity and on destabilization of areas vital to the West for geostrategic and/or resource reasons, it is essential to view the broad incursion of the Soviet Union into the area as a whole in cumulative rather than selective terms. The Soviet leadership, for the time being, has had to acquiesce in the apparent strategic stalemate that applies to

Central Europe and the northeast Pacific; however, it should be noted that the dialectic, the guiding concept of Soviet ideology, abhors prolonged stalemates and assumes that there can be only victors and losers, but no ties. Consequently, compromises can only be temporary and confined to limited portions of the globe. Therefore, the cease-fire prevailing in the areas mentioned positively requires forward movements elsewhere. In this respect, the intrinsic importance of an individual country does not matter so much as the *cumulative* impact on the perception of Third World leaders that the global "correlation of forces" is moving in favor of the Soviet Union—and that those who wish to survive had better join the bandwagon before it is too late.

In this context, others view Western unilateral withdrawals or abstentions from intervention as defeats, no less significant than actual setbacks on the battlefield. Moscow clearly offers a free hand to the national liberation movement (that is, those forces that it views as its allies), while Soviet leaders deter the "export of counterrevolution" by the West. Soviet "active measures," including disinformation and deception, are intended precisely to serve this purpose, that is, to prevent the West from counteracting the growing Soviet presence (direct or established by means of surrogates). The active measures serve to delegitimize friends and allies of the United States and to provide international respectability for the pro-Soviet forces that are attempting to weaken or annihilate such friends and allies. Efforts in the United Nations and elsewhere to write off certain countries as "pariah" states are typical of these campaigns. The intent is to make it as difficult as possible for Western governments to give meaningful assistance to friendly governments and forces.

To be sure, a good part of these battles is semantic, but only the naive and the ignorant can believe that "mere" terminology is unimportant. To mention just a few Soviet successes in this arena: Western media increasingly describe members of the Afghan resistance as "rebels," which implies, of course, that the puppet regime existing by virtue of Red Army bayonets is actually the legitimate government of Afghanistan; similarly, the forces in the field against the duly elected president and legislature of El Salvador are called anything from "guerrillas" to "freedom fighters," whereas those fighting the Sandinista regime in Nicaragua receive the dubious compliment of being described as "counter-revolutionary."

Needless to say, the same semantic battles, aided by more directly operational active measures, are also meant to legitimate Soviet intervention in such areas, whether directly or by means of proxy forces. It is particularly surprising that this game continues to be played unilaterally.

The Soviet resort to surrogates is not without its costs, since it has some destabilizing effect on the clients of the USSR who are requested to provide such services. For instance, some time ago, in connection with the activities of the contemporary Afrika Corps (that is, the proxy elements dispatched by the

GDR) the East German *Leipziger Volkszeitung* felt compelled to print a letter by a reader who asked if it would not be "more in the interest of peace and disarmament if the GDR sent no soldiers into crisis areas." The newspaper's response (that socialist countries could not permit imperialism to act at will) was not as significant, of course, as the very fact that this delicate issue had to be aired at all. Cuban ventures in the Middle East and Africa, relatively speaking, are approaching Vietnam proportions in terms of casualties and have evoked serious grumbling and unrest at home. (An autocratic regime in a closed society is more, not less, exposed to the rumor mill than open societies, since its population would take it for granted that the leadership's pronouncements are likely to be untrue; consequently, there is a greater tendency to believe gossip and rumor, however exaggerated.) This factor may not be unrelated to the boost of Soviet economic subsidies to Fidel Castro and the dispatch to Cuba of Soviet combat elements (that could act as a Praetorian Guard against popular discontent), as well as of advanced weapons, such as the MiG-23, to cover an island denuded of a considerable portion of its own armed forces.[3]

This raises the issue of why the West has done nothing to exploit such destabilizing tendencies in the home countries of the surrogate forces. The means employed need not be of a military nature at all, but rather might consist of primarily political and psychological weapons. The Chinese leaders, who detest Castro, have circulated the following riddle: "What is the largest country in the world?" Answer: "Cuba; its government is in Moscow, its armies are in Africa, and its population is . . . in Miami Beach!" This provides a rather significant key. After all, the escapees from the island include not merely adherents of the old regime or members of the underworld but some of the most notable names of the Cuban Revolution. Has it ever occurred to decisionmakers that Castro's enthusiasm for proxy operations might be cooled considerably by a hint that continued behavior along such lines could induce Western statesmen to consider recognizing a Cuban government in exile, led by the most reputable among the refugees? After all, Winston Churchill maintained in London, during World War II, any number of governments (and state councils) in exile, even if they did not control a square inch of their home territories and had very few armed men to follow them. This deprived of legitimacy regimes that rested on German bayonets, such as Pétain in Vichy, or the puppet authorities of Slovakia and Croatia. The governments in exile also offered the populations in question an ever-beckoning second option. The London-based groups included not only exiles who had been members of lawful governments prior to the German invasion, but even personalities like Dr. Beneš, who had left his country after Munich and had been succeeded by a government that was fully recognized until it too fell (to Hitler's occupation of the rump of Czechoslovakia, some five months later).

This question aside, it is necessary to emphasize that Soviet preoccupation with the Third World is not merely a contemporary phenomenon, but is solidly anchored in Leninist strategy. Since Lenin's day, the Third World has been viewed as the "reserves" of the Western societies, not merely in terms of resources, but also as the area that is "softest" as far as Soviet incursions are concerned. Consequently, the contest for global hegemony could be decided in that portion of the globe by an outflanking move that would avoid clashing frontally with Western forces where they are at their mightiest.

Lenin confronted the embarrassing fact that Marx's forecasts concerning the most advanced industrial societies were not borne out, indeed were contradicted, by events. Instead of the absolute and relative impoverishment of the proletariat in the West, leading inevitably to a socialist revolution, increased wealth provided by technological advances, plus social-reform legislation, had enabled the working class to obtain many of the benefits of increasing affluence. Lenin felt obligated to find a Marxist explanation for this unexpected phenomenon. His response was to formulate the concept of a "worker aristocracy" that had resulted, allegedly, from the "uneven development of capitalism," which had divided the world into advanced and wealthy "imperial oppressors" and poorer, disadvantaged "oppressed nations," colonies, and dependencies that constituted the "proletariat of the globe." The imperial powers, so he reasoned, were able to obtain much better returns on capital invested in colonial areas, because of the abundance of cheaper labor there. The proletarians of the metropolitan countries, consequently, could be bought off with the "crumbs" of wealth derived from exploitation of underdeveloped areas. This, he claimed, was the explanation for Marx's failure to anticipate the growth of a relatively affluent and reformist, rather than revolutionary, European "worker aristocracy."

This concept, advanced by Lenin prior to his seizure of power, was supplemented subsequently by a codicil that was to have profound impact on the conduct of Soviet operations in the Third World. Introduced at the second congress of the Comintern, and developed further by other members of that institution and by Stalin, was a new ideological construct referred to subsequently as the "national bourgeoisie." If the colonial and dependent countries were to remain sources of cheap labor, so it was argued, the imperial powers would find it counterproductive to permit the local would-be industrialists to create indigenous industries. Such enterprises would compete against the exports of the metropolitan countries and would absorb valuable raw materials needed in Europe. If this were so, the argument continued, the local national bourgeoisie was bound to struggle against the domination of imperial powers in its own self-interest, since this was the only way in which it could attain industrial status. Consequently, a two-stage revolution could be anticipated in the colonial and dependent countries. In the first phase the national bourgeoisie would make common cause with the "masses" (some rural and some urban, but not yet genuinely "proletarian") to drive out foreign domination; the Soviet "motherland of the revolution" would give full military, as well as ideological, support to these colonial fighters, even though they would be neither communist nor proletarian. Moreover, even where local Communist parties existed (in as yet embryonic form), they should be supporters and followers of the national bourgeois leadership. The Communists should suffer quietly if their temporary allies, unwilling to brook opposition (particularly from elements tied to a foreign power), refused to permit the legal existence of a Marxist-Leninist party and went so far as to liquidate individual Communists.

Once the imperial power had been ousted, however, the national bourgeoisie would proceed, obviously, to construct its own industries. At that point it would become a reactionary class, replicating an earlier period of European history. This would initiate the second stage of the colonial revolution, in which the indigenous proletariat, an inevitable by-product of the newly created industries, would rise up against its erstwhile allies. There was just one little snag in this elaborate theory, namely, that it expected Communist parties in the colonies to suffer suppression meekly during the first stage and to go on supporting their bourgeois allies. How could they do so, knowing full well that, during the second stage, the Communists were expected to shed their blood on the barricades built by elements brought to power with the aid not only of the local communist organizations, but of Soviet advisers, instructors, rifles, and artillery? Not surprisingly, many Asian Communists, such as M. N. Roy and leading members of the Chinese Communist Party, remonstrated repeatedly against this Comintern concept, which they regarded as self-defeating and, indeed, as opportunistic rather than revolutionary.

To Moscow, however, the desire of Asian Communists to lead colonial revolutionary movements from their very inception appeared unrealistic and even undesirable. Communist parties in the Third World were minuscule, with some minor exceptions, and attracted little mass following, certainly when compared with genuine movements supported by Lenin and Stalin, especially the Kuomintang (KMT) in China. Comintern support for purely communist elements, Moscow feared, would merely drive nationalist organizations into a rapprochement with the imperial powers. The result might be relative calm rather than destabilization in the colonial possessions of the Kremlin's "principal antagonist," namely Great Britain. Lenin and Stalin were convinced, during the initial period of Soviet rule, that, as a relatively weak power, the Soviet state could not afford to tackle its adversaries frontally but would have to rely on diversionary tactics, such as indirectly promoting instability in the colonial areas. This had the added virtue, moreover, of creating ferment in parts of the globe in which the imperial powers were notoriously at odds with one another, so that one could play off, for instance, Great Britain against France.

Lenin, indeed, postulated that, by depriving the rulers of the European powers of their colonial reserves, one could render them incapable of "trickling down" the wealth obtained from their overseas possessions to their worker aristocracy. As a result, the workers would be impoverished and would change from a reformist to a revolutionary element. Thus, colonial struggles for independence might precipitate a belated socialist revolution in Europe. This, apparently, was the basis for the introduction of the slogan that "the road to Paris (or London) runs through Canton (or Calcutta)."

There was an even more compelling consideration, namely, that "the chain of imperialism may be broken at its weakest link." In effect, this meant that whereas in Europe the "bourgeois state" had established itself with a very strong infrastructure, including a large and supportive middle class and all the modern, technological appurtenances of power, in the Third World minuscule elites could be penetrated easily and influenced through a handful of key personalities. Without the presence and support of a sizable middle class or any of the other essential elements for the exercise and preservation of power, Third World regimes could be taken over or removed. In this sense, the colonial and dependent countries truly constituted the weakest link. These were the reasons why Lenin eventually went so far as to amend the famous slogan of the Communist Manifesto from "workers of all countries unite" to "workers of all countries and oppressed nations unite."

The new slogan, however, carried implications that became explicit very soon. Lenin had not only replaced the Marxist concept of class struggle within countries with class struggle between states (an international class struggle, as it were), but he had proceeded to blame the Third World's disadvantages on the *proletariat*, as well as the ruling classes, of the imperial powers. Lenin, of course, was bitterly disappointed that the prestigious, mass European socialist parties had failed to accept his leadership or his ideology. The result, however, was that the predominantly socioeconomic Marxist approach soon was tinged with Leninist ethnic, and even racial, overtones. In the case of Turkey, for instance, Moscow came to support the Kemalist military forces as representing the "progressive" (national) bourgeoisie, and the question arose as to who, in that case, constituted the "reactionary" forces ("comprador bourgeoisie"). Lenin came up with the original idea that, in Turkey, the compradors simply were the Greeks and the Armenians! Other elements within the Bolshevik leadership (for instance, Stalin's protégé, Sultan-Galiev) took this approach one step further by insisting that Asians, irrespective of class, were innately more progressive than Europeans. Four decades later, therefore, Mao had good sources for his theory of the "intermediate zone," which posited that the whole nonwhite world was fundamentally more revolutionary than the areas populated by whites.

Other inherent problems became evident as well. Most of the countries to which the Leninist formula was applied were not actual colonies, but rather semidependent states like Turkey, Iran, Afghanistan, and China. Consequently, the whole concept of the second stage of the colonial revolution was highly questionable. After all, the national movement in such countries did not have to fight for independence. At least formally, these were sovereign entities, even if their sovereignty was somewhat circumscribed (for instance, by the capitulations system). Essentially, therefore, they were arenas of combat between rival movements of a predominantly military rather than bourgeois character (for example, those led by Kemal Atatürk, Reza Pahlavi, and Chiang Kai-shek), and their aims related less to industrialization than to modern secular nationalism. The whole scenario, consequently, of a first stage to oust the imperial power and a second stage to overthrow the newly established industrial bourgeoisie was inapplicable. Moreover, Moscow's new allies in the Third World were perfectly capable of reading the operational details of the program for the colonial and dependent areas that the Comintern had prepared and published rather candidly and prominently. Obviously, the national bourgeoisie was aware of the fate envisaged for it in the second stage, when its temporary communist allies were supposed to support it "as the rope supports the hanged man." Neither Chiang nor Kemal were inclined to wait for that second stage, and they took the appropriate measures, of a rather final nature, to deal with the indigenous Communist parties.

This created (and continues to create, even today) some dilemmas for a Soviet state that is supposed to be the "motherland of the socialist revolution"— and, indeed, derives its only form of legitimation from this claim. Soviet leaders have had to choose constantly between continued support for national movements in developing areas, thus frequently abandoning their communist comrades to a brutal fate (with consequent fallout on Moscow's standing within the international communist movement), and a sudden reversal of the alliance with the national bourgeoisie, with resulting loss of leverage and investments (military, economic, and political) in the countries concerned.

From a very early stage onward, the Kremlin realized that, ideological rhetoric notwithstanding, its allies in the Third World were predominantly military officers. Soviet assistance, therefore, had to take primarily military form, including staff and technical training and weapons transfers—the creation of Whampoa Academy and the Borodin Mission offer good illustrations of this approach. Embarrassingly for Moscow, these weapons could be and occasionally were used against indigenous Communists, although, on the positive side, such operations had obvious implications for Soviet intelligence and the infiltration of moles.

On the whole, Moscow has preferred to tell its communist comrades to "grin and bear it" (as Radek told a Turkish communist delegation complaining about Kemalist liquidation tactics) and has continued support for selected leaders of colonial national movements. This has created an obvious ideological difficulty, however. If the national bourgeoisie continued to receive Soviet assistance beyond the first stage of the colonial revolution, then the question arose as to when, if ever, the second stage would be initiated and when the time would be deemed right for a socialist revolution. Moscow's answer to this problem was "the noncapitalist path of development." In simple English, this meant that the second stage might never be necessary; the national movement, once it was in power, would implement development through radical reforms leading toward socialism, by-passing the capitalist stage altogether. What was to compel it to act in this manner? Not the indigenous proletariat, which was likely to remain weak (particularly in view of repeated purges at the hands of the national leaders), but rather the "international proletariat," as personified by "the motherland of the socialist revolution," that is, the Soviet Union.

Substituting for the feeble local proletariat, the Soviet leadership, with its hands on the pipeline of military and other assistance, would cajole and coerce national leaders in the Third World to take the desired measures. This was hardly compatible with orthodox Marxism, but then Lenin, when challenged by colleagues who pointed out the contradiction between his operational tactics and the concepts of the Communist Manifesto, very candidly admitted that "conditions have changed" and that a different approach was essential to exploit existing situations. A less kind term for Lenin's posture, of course, was simply "opportunism."

There are interesting, tantalizing signs that the Lenin-Stalin concept of Third World operations has periodically encountered misgivings within the ranks of the Soviet leadership. In the mid-1920s, for instance, Stalin referred obliquely to colleagues who had suggested that, instead of Soviet support for national movements in the colonial and dependent areas, Moscow ought to make agreements with the imperial powers to divide China, Turkey, and others into spheres of influence. Although Stalin mentioned this idea critically, his practice, at least in China, could be categorized easily under the same heading. Side by side with the rather intimate Soviet-KMT relationship, the Kremlin maintained all kinds of ties with various warlords in China's northern and northeastern regions, as well as with the weak Peking government, just as Britain, for instance, also had its contacts with various, mutually incompatible, Chinese elements. On the "left," both Trotsky and some of the Asian communist leaders vigorously opposed the concept of supporting national bourgeois movements instead of indigenous Communists.

Stalin himself burdened his policy and the communist movement in the Third World with serious political liabilities. In the 1920s, he persisted stubbornly with his KMT links, despite the resulting decimation of the Chinese Communist Party, possibly because he thought that abandoning his policy in the face of Trotsky's attacks would imply a confession of error. By 1927–1928, however, Stalin could no longer deny that his obstinacy had resulted in a fiasco; he switched to the other extreme, namely, a far "leftist" approach. The new line denounced not only the national bourgeoisie but even the "petty bourgeoisie," that is, small traders, artisans, students, and teachers, who, in the Comintern's scenario, had been viewed always as potential long-term allies who would remain "progressive" even during the second stage of the colonial revolution. The result of Stalin's turnabout was that the indigenous Asian communist leaders indulged in a frenzied campaign of verbal abuse of such venerated national figures as Gandhi, a behavior pattern that was not soon forgotten (above all, because it presented the Asian nationalist movements with a two-front battle—against the representatives of the imperial power on the right and against the Communists on the left).

Subsequently, the offense was aggravated during two of Stalin's sudden lurches to the "right," namely, the "Popular Front" years (1935–1938) and the "Grand Coalition" period (1941–1945). During the former, Mao was told in rather peremptory tones to resume the alliance with the KMT, much to his resentment; during the latter (much more damaging in the long run), Communists in the colonies were told to adopt the slogan "All for the War," which entailed denunciation of "fascist" national leaders who did not agree to cease the struggle for independence (against such imperial powers as Britain, from which invaluable military assistance was flowing to the Red Army). In fact, the Indian Communists became the strongest and most consistent defenders of the British raj, a posture not easily forgotten or forgiven by Asian nationalists. This blemish became more evident still as a result of the behavior of the French Communist Party during the immediate post–World War II period, when it participated in the French coalition cabinet and became noticeably lukewarm vis-à-vis independence movements that threatened to tear away sizable chunks from the French Union.

Such erratic behavior and opportunism left a long-lasting odor. It was not dissipated by the fact that the countries of South and Southeast Asia had no sooner attained independence than the Communist parties launched a series of bloody, albeit unsuccessful, insurrections in 1948.

Soviet practice, both during the Comintern period and subsequently, underlined the perception that the very structure of the international communist movement reflected imperial patterns. In the 1930s, for instance, guidance of the Indian Communist Party emanated from a section of the British Communist Party, headed by R. Palme Dutt. For a time, the Indonesian Communist Party was run by a Dutchman. Subsequently, the French Communist Party was placed in charge of communist organizations throughout the non-European sectors of the Mediterranean littoral. Only in 1950, so informants from the Italian Communist Party report, did Stalin decide that the French Communists had so blotted their copybook with regard to Africa and Asia as to require the transfer of their authority in the Mediterranean region to another organization. The lucky recipient of this responsibility was the Italian Communist Party (PCI), which, by good fortune, had been spared the temptation to follow the imperial patterns of the British and French Communist parties. (The PCI was outlawed, of course, during the period of Mussolini's African empire, and when the party entered the Italian coalition government at the end of World War II, Allied forces had just stripped Italy of all her colonial possessions.) Consequently, the PCI was placed in charge of Communist parties on the southern and eastern shores of the Mediterranean and, subsequently, of "fraternal" noncommunist organizations, such as the Algerian FLN, the Egyptian ASU, and the Syrian Ba'ath. (In later years, of course, Fidel Castro was given similar status vis-à-vis leftist elements throughout the Caribbean.)

These organizational oddities do not mean that the Soviet central apparatus was not at all times the court of last resort as far as major changes of course were concerned. The Comintern was an integral part of that apparatus, obviously, until its formal dissolution in 1943. It was succeeded by the International Department (under various names) of the Secretariat of the Central Committee of the CPSU. In the post–World War II period, with the appearance of additional communist states, that department eventually divided its functions between two sections—one in charge of the relationship between the CPSU and ruling Communist parties and the other, more directly relevant for the Third World, supervised relations with nonruling Communist parties (and, eventually, with other fraternal parties of the left, some of which seized power in the newly independent countries).

Despite repeated assertions to the contrary, during Stalin's last years, when Zhdanov was in the ascendancy, the Soviet leadership did not display indifference toward the Third World. Indeed, Zhdanov's famous address to the founding meeting of the Cominform, in September of 1947, devoted particular attention to five countries in that part of the globe—Indonesia, Indochina, India, Egypt, and Syria. Zhdanov's adversary, E. Varga, developed a theory that former colonies could attain independence by means short of violent revolution and struggle since, as suppliers of raw material to the imperial powers during World War II, they had become creditors and, as such, could extort independence in lieu of repayment of debts, which the metropolitan powers were no longer able to afford.

The Cominform itself, unlike its predecessor, the Comintern, does not appear to have had formal jurisdiction over the colonial areas. After its dissolution in 1957, a new, somewhat looser communist framework was established. It operated through the editorial offices of the new journal, *Problems of Peace and Socialism*, in Prague (which served not only as an organizational center for Third World affairs, but also as a place of exile for left-wing leaders whose parties had been outlawed).

Although a great deal of ideological and operational innovation has been attributed to N. S. Khrushchev, most of his concepts concerning the Third

World, including his very terminology, were drawn lock, stock, and barrel from the glossary of the Comintern period. Khrushchev's interest in the Third World seems to have been due, in the first place, to his desire to mold and manipulate global perceptions. The Soviet preoccupation with size and numbers played an important role in this context. Stalin had conjured up the image of "the socialist sixth of the world," conveniently overlooking the fact that most of this sixth consisted of permafrost and, in terms of population, it was more like one-twelfth of the world. After Eastern Europe and China became part of the bloc, Khrushchev opportunistically switched the frame of reference from area to population and spoke of "the socialist third of mankind." Toward the end of the 1950s, however, he began to feel that the correlation of forces was swinging in favor of the USSR. To furbish this trend with the appropriate image, Khrushchev coined the term "the zone of peace," consisting of "two-thirds of mankind"—simply subsuming all of the decolonized areas under one heading with the communist bloc. Like the Hungarian leader, János Kádár, Khrushchev decided to reverse Lenin's dictum and to assume that "he who is not against us, is for us." Since "nonalignment" increasingly was becoming the favored slogan of the Third World, it became legitimate, in Khrushchev's eyes, to include these countries on his side of the ledger.

Obviously, this entailed evolving an operational framework for the Third World that encompassed military supply relationships, high visibility assistance projects, and suitable adjustments in Moscow's ideological approach. The latter was accomplished by extracting from the Comintern glossary the concepts of the "national democratic movement" and the "noncapitalist path of development." The former, with one slight adaptation—from "national democratic movement" to "national democracy" (since many of these movements had attained state power in the meantime)—was defined as a four-class coalition of the national bourgeoisie (the leader) and the petty bourgeoisie, the peasants, and the proletariat (mere followers). The concept of the "two-stage colonial revolution" was amended (the first stage, gaining independence by ousting the imperial power, having been attained). References to the second stage were tacitly deleted, on the grounds that the violent overthrow of the national bourgeoisie by the proletariat would be unnecessary. The former, with the aid of the "international proletariat"—represented by the Soviet state, the supplier of military and technological assistance—was capable of initiating the non-capitalist path of development that would lead eventually to socialism, without first passing through a capitalist phase.

This meant, in fact, conferring the support of the international communist movement on certain newly independent countries led by noncommunists. Nominal conditions were attached, to be sure, that these regimes should implement radical reform measures, particularly in the agrarian sector; that the local Communist parties should be permitted to organize; and, most importantly, that these countries should pursue a pro-Soviet, anti-Western, foreign policy. Few of these "national democracies," being mostly single-party states, were prepared to grant rival parties (least of all organizations with ties to an outside power) the right to organize, indeed to exist, and Moscow seems to have resigned itself to this situation without too much fuss. The whole concept of national democracy was considered a sufficiently permanent feature of Soviet policy to be canonized, as it were, by enshrinement in the 1961 CPSU party program, as part of a special section on the national liberation movement.

Khrushchev went one step further by granting the ruling (single) parties of these Third World countries candidate status, so to speak, in the international communist movement. He included them as fraternal guests at gatherings that had been limited heretofore to Communists, such as the twenty-second CPSU congress in 1961. Starting with the ruling parties of Ghana, Guinea, and Mali, this privilege was extended subsequently to the FLN of Algeria, the ASU of Egypt, the Ba'ath of Syria, and others. Although this practice was relatively unproblematical with regard to states containing only minuscule Communist parties, it became fraught with difficulties in cases where relatively important Communist parties existed. Thus, at the twenty-third CPSU congress in 1966, Brezhnev attempted to walk a tightrope by welcoming simultaneously the representatives of Algeria's FLN and "communist comrades from Algeria," that is, individual Communists rather than the Algerian Communist Party (which, to all intents and purposes, had been outlawed by the FLN). This attempt at evenhandedness succeeded only in enraging both—the FLN because it was not granted monopoly status and Algerian Communists were mentioned at all, and the Algerian Communist Party because only its individual members were acknowledged, delegitimizing the party as a whole.

The list of Third World countries included in this category varied, of course, from time to time, particularly since the regimes patronized by Moscow occasionally were alienated, as was Guinea's leader after 1961, or overthrown, as was Ghana's Nkrumah in 1966. In several instances, the USSR suffered setbacks in countries in which it had issued fewer and fewer caveats regarding the treatment of indigenous Communists. In the late 1950s, Khrushchev had still protested against anticommunist restrictions in the national democracies, and he had stressed that their respective ideologies ("African socialism," "Arab socialism") were not "scientific" socialism (Marxism-Leninism). Whatever their wishes, eventually they would have to embrace the genuine article and become Communists. By the 1960s, such reservations were heard less and less. Indeed, Khrushchev soon dug up another term from the Comintern glossary, "revolutionary democrats." The same Third World leaders who had been classified previously as members of the national bourgeoisie (a class temporarily progressive, but destined eventually to become reactionary) were now rebaptized and defined as members of the petty bourgeoisie or as revolutionary democrats, a progressive element that could be relied upon to remain friendly for an indefinite period of time.

The publicists patronized by Khrushchev, particularly in the Institute of World Economics and International Relations (IMEiMO, which became authoritative on matters pertaining to the Third World), acknowledged that Moscow's clients in the developing countries were not would-be industrialists, as had been assumed since Lenin's time, but rather were members of an element recognized for the first time as a class, namely, military officers. As such, they were viewed as predominantly of petty bourgeois or peasant origin. Although they might tend to vacillate, such elements could be disciplined through the exercise of vigilant supervision by the international proletariat (that is, the Soviet state) and could become and remain reliable allies. The real reason for this earth-shaking (but hardly Marxist) discovery was the appearance of Fidel Castro. Moscow had found, somewhat to its surprise, that a guerrilla leader, sometimes at odds with the orthodox Cuban Communist Party, had come to power and had "subjectively" declared himself to be a genuine Marxist-Leninist. Subsequently he had performed as if he really were what he claimed to be. Moscow's agenda, therefore, became the search for more Castros and, in this effort, "objective" criteria of a class and ideological nature were thrown overboard, more and more, in favor of operational, opportunistic considerations. Thus, if Colonel Nasser was promoted from affiliation with the national bourgeoisie to membership in the petty bourgeoisie (or officer class), then his country also had to be upgraded from a national democracy to a revolutionary democracy. Moscow, it should be noted, imposed even fewer restrictions on the latter than on the former. The Soviet leaders no longer required that the local Communist Party be granted the right to organize, but merely asked that individual Communists be spared persecution, so as not to embarrass the Soviet Union (in its role as the center of the international communist movement). Needless to say, even the latter, much more modest, request was not always met, and Moscow chose not to make this too much of an issue. The same forbearance, however, could not be expected from the local Communists, some of whom, such as the prominent Syrian communist leader, Khaled Bagdash, openly criticized the Soviet leadership for its unwavering support of Middle Eastern military dictators.

Asian and African communist leaders, however, were not alone in their misgivings. At least one portion of the Soviet leadership voiced reservations about Khrushchev's overenthusiastic approach to his newly discovered partners in the Third World. Those in charge of the foreign relations of the CPSU, especially Suslov and Ponomarev, were concerned, not unnaturally, that their "constituents"—that is, the indigenous Communists—were being sacrificed in favor of national leaders in the countries concerned. The political (indeed, physical) longevity of these rulers was far from assured, and their gratitude was unlikely to last from one day to the next. These doubts were substantiated in such instances as the break with Sekou Touré in 1961 and Kwame Nkrumah's overthrow in 1966. Moreover, there were other members of the Soviet regime who were notably cool toward what they viewed as an overexpenditure of Soviet resources on such showpieces as the Jakarta Sports Palace or the Aswan Dam. The anti–foreign aid lobby in Moscow appears to have gathered sufficient steam, at one time, for Khrushchev to have felt impelled to force some of its members to confess, at the twenty-first CPSU congress in 1959, that they had opposed "helping the partly developed and developing countries of Asia and the Near East" and had "behaved like people blinded by narrow-minded national insularism." After Khrushchev's overthrow, *Pravda* carried articles reminding readers that Lenin had always emphasized investment in more, rather than less, developed areas, since that was the best way of obtaining a rapid return. In the long run, Lenin had argued, making developed regions more viable was the best way of enabling them to assist the underdeveloped areas!

Dissident voices, however, were also heard from another quarter, namely, the People's Republic of China. Clearly, the Chinese leaders felt that, rather than frittering away Soviet and East European resources on countries outside the bloc, with results that were unlikely to be decisive, Moscow would do much better to concentrate whatever surpluses it might have on China. Substantial aid would enable Beijing to make a qualitative leap forward, bringing the country at least to the level of the East European states. To be sure, the Chinese leaders could be just as opportunistic as Moscow, nor were they necessarily more doctrinaire in their dealings with the Third World. Indeed, in one of the acrimonious exchanges between the two capitals in the early 1960s, the Chinese leadership praised even "kings, princes, and aristocrats" in developing countries, provided these forces pursued an appropriate foreign poicy (as had Morocco, when its king offered a safe base to the Algerian FLN members who were fighting the French). Beijing, however, though perfectly prepared to collaborate with such elements, was unwilling to follow in Soviet footsteps by giving an ideological imprimatur to noncommunists.

The East European countries (particularly Czechoslovakia), forced to act as funnels for Soviet military shipments to various clients in the Third World, were even less enthusiastic. They found various subtle ways to indicate that the recipients were less than grateful and expected a great deal without being willing to provide an adequate return.

As this survey indicates, therefore, evolving Soviet policy toward the Third World has not been devoid of tactical and ideological problems. Such difficulties, however, are offset by the geopolitical and perceptual advantages the Soviet hegemonial drive has reaped. The USSR's patient, yet relentless, penetration of this sector of the globe has cost relatively little. Military and security arrangements that induce the small elites of such countries to "vibrate in harmony" with the USSR obviously are considered by Moscow to be more important than ideological purity or consistency. The cumulative impact of an ever larger number of countries joining this broad category (if only as measured by voting patterns in the U.N. General Assembly) creates a general perception of Soviet momentum. The USSR hopes to benefit from a worldwide impression that a qualitative change is occurring in the correlation of forces that will be the hallmark of the third (and final) stage in the general crisis of world capitalism—a stage that will mean (so Leninist doctrine claims) an *irreversible* transformation in the balance of power.

The truth of the matter is that Moscow has swallowed occasional setbacks and simply has persisted until the situation was reversed, whereas the West, in most instances, has lacked the same degree of patience, determination, and relentlessness and has only a few Grenadas to show on its side of the ledger. In this connection, there are certain optical illusions; for instance, the textbooks teach us to regard the Cuban missile crisis as a classic case of Western diplomacy compelling the USSR to "blink first." Overlooked is the fact that the USSR succeeded in its primary objective, namely the implantation in the western hemisphere of a pro-Soviet state in close proximity to the United States. Cuba has served not only as a facility for Soviet naval and air elements but also as a base area from which activities can be organized to extend the Soviet sphere to include portions of the Central American mainland. In this sense, the Brezhnev Doctrine, the concept of the irreversibility of the installation of pro-Soviet regimes, not merely in Eastern Europe, but even in our hemisphere, appears to have been accepted as valid by the West—surely a major retreat.

NOTES

1. The analysis regarding the role of the 1972–1973 Soviet-American agreements as factors in initiating the contemporary phase in Moscow's use of surrogates was presented in the late Gavriel D. Ra'anan's chapter on "Surrogate Forces and Power Projection," in U. Ra'anan, R. L. Pfaltzgraff, and G. Kemp, eds., *Projection of Power* (Hamden, Conn.: Archon Books, 1982).

2. Ibid., pp. 284–85.

3. Ibid., p. 284.

The Nature of the Problem: A Systematic Soviet Strategy for the Third World?

Francis Fukuyama

INTRODUCTION

Over much of the postwar period the Third World has constituted the chief arena of East-West competition, and it promises to remain so for the foreseeable future. The extraordinary burst of Soviet activism that began with the October 1973 Middle East war and culminated in the invasion of Afghanistan was responsible, more than any other factor, for American disillusionment with détente and the subsequent broad decline in U.S.-Soviet relations. There is, however, considerable disagreement over the significance of Soviet behavior and the extent to which it represents a systematic strategy on the part of Moscow. At the poles of this perennial debate lie two opposing views. The first, which enjoyed something of a revival following the invasion of Afghanistan, maintains that Moscow's moves in the Third World reflect a carefully thought-out long-term military strategy for achieving certain fairly specific objectives like access to warm-water ports or control over oil, with the Soviets playing a major role in initiating and promoting local conflicts. The second, by contrast, tends to dismiss the idea that the Soviets are pursuing a coherent military strategy, believing instead that their behavior reflects simple opportunism. According to this view, Third World instabilities are primarily manifestations of local condi-

© Council on Foreign Relations. This paper is based on a presentation entitled "The Military Dimension of Soviet Policy in the Third World," presented in connection with a Council Working Group on the "Soviet 'Extended Empire.'" The views expressed in this paper do not necessarily reflect those of the Rand Corporation or its sponsors.

tions over which the Soviets have little control, and they are most often used by Soviet clients for their own purposes.

One does not need to posit anything like Soviet omniscience or total control over events to see coherent elements in Soviet behavior. The answer to the question of whether the Soviets have a *systematic strategy* for the Third World depends entirely on how the term is defined. If it implies a grand strategy for achieving specific territorial objectives on a fixed timetable in the manner of Hitler's Hossbach Memorandum, in which plans for the conquest of certain countries were laid out, then the answer is almost certainly no. The major Soviet advances of the past decade have generally come about as a result of successful Soviet exploitation of opportunities created in local contexts, rather than through a plan thought out and initiated in advance.[1]

For example, Moscow's current presence in the Horn of Africa had its origins in the drought in Ethiopia in 1973–1974 and the monarchy's incompetent response to the resulting conditions of famine. Although the Soviets aggressively moved to exploit the opening that this disaster provided, thereby deepening and prolonging the conflict within Ethiopia and between the country and its neighbors, the USSR would not have been able to initiate the collapse of the old regime on its own. The same is true for Soviet advances in Angola and Mozambique, which were made possible by the revolution in Portugal and Lisbon's decision to grant its former colonies independence.[2] Anyone familiar with regions like the Middle East and Africa will realize that long-term strategic planning is virtually impossible for either superpower to achieve or implement given the extreme instability of local politics and the weakness of most of the superpowers' instruments of leverage.

If, however, systematic strategy means the pursuit of a consistent strategic aim—such as access to military facilities, the steady undermining of Western positions, and the accretion of Soviet influence—and a set of coherent tactical principles (as opposed to detailed plans) for achieving them, then the Soviet Union may in fact have such a strategy. It is possible to uncover a number of systematic patterns in Soviet behavior, with regard to both objectives and the tactical principles used for achieving them. Both have been evolving steadily over the years. Whereas a good deal of Soviet behavior in the Third World from the mid-1950s through the early 1970s could be explained in terms of Moscow's search for geostrategic positions of concrete military value, for the most part related to its strategic nuclear posture, the most important Soviet objectives were achieved by the end of that period. Although still concerned with geostrategic position, Moscow's emphasis over the past decade has turned much more to the problem of improving the quality of its influence in existing positions, rather than simply expanding its influence. Indeed, one can make a case that Soviet tactics for acquiring and maintaining Third World clients underwent a major revision in the mid-1970s, and that the Soviets have developed a fairly elaborate system for dealing with the problem of client unreliability that plagued much of their policy in the Third World in the 1950s and 1960s. These are trends that are likely to continue in the future.

THE HISTORICAL EVOLUTION OF SOVIET STRATEGIC OBJECTIVES

On the most general level, one could characterize Soviet objectives in the Third World as the greatest possible expansion of Soviet interests and influence at the expense of those of the West, particularly the United States. Influence is a fungible commodity, somewhat like money in the bank, which is valuable in its own right but also convertible into concrete assets like bases or facilities. It is possible, however, to be much more specific about Soviet goals, since military objectives, and particularly the requirements generated by Moscow's strategic nuclear posture, have played a major role in establishing the overall scope and direction of Soviet expansion in the Third World. The character of these interests has changed over time. The strategic nuclear dimension assumed relatively greater importance in the first three postwar decades than subsequently. We therefore need to look at Soviet policy in a more concrete historical context.

In the immediate aftermath of World War II, the Soviets were not preoccupied with a strategic requirement for overseas bases; indeed, they withdrew from Porkala Udd in Finland and Port Arthur and Dairen in China in the interests of better relations with the countries concerned. By the time of Moscow's turn toward the Third World during the 1950s, however, Soviet policy was directly shaped by concerns related to the strategic nuclear balance. The United States at that time was seeking to erect a strategic containment barrier through the establishment of a series of interlocking defensive pacts with nations on the periphery of the USSR. The repeated attempts to organize the countries of the northern tier into various pro-Western alliances like the Baghdad Pact and CENTO were a part of this effort. Underlying these alliances was a very concrete military rationale: given the relatively limited ranges of early strategic systems (that is, medium-range B-47 bombers, intermediate-range ballistic missiles [IRBMs], and carrier-based aviation), implementation of the Dulles-era massive retaliation strategy required a network of bases and intelligence facilities close to the Soviet Union. Without denying the role of chance and opportunism, one important motive for Moscow's cultivation of Nasser and its subsequent establishment of ties with a number of important Arab states was to find a way of neutralizing U.S. strategic assets in the northern tier, particularly in Iraq. Khrushchev appears to have regarded Egypt and Syria initially as bargaining chips, and he called repeatedly for a great-power conference on the Middle East that in effect would have traded the Soviet position in the Middle Eastern heartland for Western positions in the northern tier.[3]

The pattern of Soviet involvement in the Third World from the early 1960s to the early 1970s also had a more or less coherent strategic rationale. The Soviet objective of disrupting the Baghdad Pact was largely achieved with the Iraqi revolution in 1958, and the importance to the United States of regions on the periphery of the USSR declined with the development of ICBMs and long-range bombers (U.S. IRBMs in Turkey, for example, were unilaterally withdrawn following the Cuban missile crisis). Changes in naval technology created two new missions for the Soviet navy: first, to deploy and protect its own first- and second-generation ballistic-missile-carrying submarines (SSBNs) in forward patrol areas near the U.S. coastline and, second, to counter U.S. missile-carrying submarines in their forward-deployment areas.[4] In addition, range increases in American carrier-based aircraft now permitted the United States to deliver nuclear strikes against Soviet territory from areas like the eastern Mediterranean. The deployment of a permanent Soviet naval squadron in the Mediterranean after 1964 for antisubmarine warfare (ASW) and anticarrier missions generated a substantial overseas basing requirement. Hence, the inherent importance of countries like Egypt, Syria, and Algeria grew in Soviet eyes as the USSR began to search around the Mediterranean littoral for support facilities. More distant countries like Cuba, Somalia, Guinea, and South Yemen (the People's Democratic Republic of Yemen, or PDRY) offered similar support opportunities for forward-deployed Soviet submarines.[5]

It should be noted, of course, that these strategic calculations can account for only a part of Soviet policy toward the Third World during either the 1950s or the 1960s. Moscow's assiduous cultivation of India or Indonesia during the 1950s, for example, was totally unrelated to the nuclear balance, as was its grooming in the 1960s of clients like Mali, Nigeria, or the Congo.

What are we to make of the numerous and varied Soviet Third World activities from 1975 to the present? Although I think one can uncover a systematic pattern in recent Soviet tactics, it is a bit harder to detect a unifying pattern with regard to ends. Certainly China constituted one important theme: once war with the People's Republic became a real possibility after 1969, Soviet planners had to take seriously the problem of maintaining sea lines of communication to the Soviet Far East. This helps to explain a good deal of Moscow's interest in the Indian Ocean and the quest for facilities in places like Ethiopia and the PDRY. Vietnam not only provided facilities for reconnaissance and forces forward-deployed in the Indian Ocean, but was itself a substantial military counterweight to China. Finally, Moscow's intense courtship of India, particularly after the invasion of Afghanistan in late 1979, was designed to keep China encircled from the south.

It is fairly clear that considerations related to the strategic nuclear balance played a considerably smaller role in the 1970s than in the previous two decades. In large measure this was because Moscow had successfully achieved its earlier objectives: U.S. strategic systems were driven away from its periphery, and forward naval deployments in critical areas like the Mediterranean and Indian oceans were implemented with the acquisition of basing facilities in Egypt, Syria, Algeria, and Somalia. Technological improvements in Soviet submarine-launched missile ranges allowed the USSR to move to bastion defense of its SSBN fleet in nearby protected oceans like the Barents Sea or the Sea of Okhotsk, thus reducing requirements for long-range forward deployments.[6] Similarly, the range of American submarine-launched ballistic missiles (SLBMs) improved and vastly expanded the ocean areas in which U.S. submarines could patrol. Since the Soviets were never able to develop significant open-ocean ASW capabilities, they began to reach a point of diminishing marginal returns with regard to this mission.[7]

Throughout the postwar period, the Soviets have never been reluctant to press their clients hard for access to military facilities. Sadat and Heikal, for example, both document the strong and consistent pressure brought to bear on Egypt for access to naval facilities. The Soviets reportedly held out stubbornly for access to Cam Ranh Bay during their negotiations with the Vietnamese on the 1978 friendship treaty. Nevertheless, the Soviets have consistently maintained a relatively long-term view of their interests and have frequently subordinated immediate military goals to other concerns, for example, the desire to expand their general fund of political influence in a particular country. Moscow has never made access to facilities a sine qua non of support for otherwise sympathetic clients, and the USSR has proven willing to sink enormous amounts of money into clients who had no immediate prospects of direct military payoff (for example, India and North Yemen).[8] Indeed, Moscow's courtship of Ethiopia in 1977–1978 indicated that although the Soviets had a long-term strategic view of the importance of the Horn of Africa, they were willing to risk the sacrifice, at least in the short run, of a concrete military asset—the naval facility at Berbera—for the sake of the vaguer goal of increased political influence.[9]

A SYSTEMATIC STRATEGY IN THE 1970s?

Although the achievement of specific strategic objectives has been less of a driving force behind Soviet policy in the Third World in the past decade, the tactical principles employed by Moscow for gaining and holding on to influence have shifted markedly. The value of a given client is the product of two separate factors: first, its objective political and military value to the Soviet Union, measured in terms of size, resources, geostrategic position, population, and so on and, second, the quality of Soviet influence over the state in question, including the durability of the Soviet presence and the client's willingness to act militarily on behalf of Soviet interests or to permit Soviet forces to operate from its territory. Although the quantity of Soviet clients expanded dramatically between 1955 and the early seventies, in many cases the quality of Moscow's relationships left much to be desired. Soviet tactics for improving the quality of influence therefore underwent a major revision toward the middle of the decade, the results of which we are currently witnessing.[10]

The reasons for this revision lay in the inherent weaknesses of the USSR's state-to-state dealings with its Third World clients before the early 1970s. Khrushchev's major innovation with regard to Third World policy was to reduce the emphasis on orthodox Communist parties, characteristic of the Stalin era, and to increase contacts with left-wing but noncommunist nationalist regimes in the developing world. This policy was announced at the twentieth party congress in 1956 but had been put into practice the year before via the famous arms deal with Nasser. The policy was underwritten primarily by arms transfers and secondarily by economic aid and promises of political and military assistance in conflicts with the West—the latter honored more often than not in the breach. The new policy was responsible for an enormous expansion in Soviet influence throughout the Third World over the next two decades, but it brought a host of problems. The types of regimes courted turned out to be unstable, nationalistic, and, as a consequence, politically unreliable. Furthermore, arms transfers proved to be an extremely weak instrument of leverage. In many instances the entire Soviet position in a particular country rested on the fate of a single leader at the top (like Sukarno, Keita, Nkrumah, or Sadat) whose death, overthrow, or defection could have disastrous consequences for the Soviets. Many clients such as Syria were able to extract enormous amounts of aid from Moscow for many years while resisting basic Soviet wishes (in this case, Syria postponed signature of a friendship treaty until 1980). In many cases Moscow's desire to cultivate good relations with a ruling nationalist regime has led it to tolerate the brutal suppression of local Communists, as happened in Egypt and Syria in the late 1950s and in Iraq in 1959 and again in 1977.[11] Only Cuba (and possibly the PDRY) followed the path of "natural" development from bourgeois nationalist regimes into more or less orthodox Marxist-Leninist ones.

The problems Moscow encountered with noncommunist bourgeois regimes are probably best illustrated by the case of Egypt. Following Egypt's defeat in the June 1967 war, the Soviets found themselves drawn deeper and deeper into the conflict. They deployed nearly 20,000 combat forces in that country by 1970 and yet were unable to control the behavior of their client in many crucial respects. The Soviets attempted to manipulate arms deliveries in such a way as to maintain their standing with Egypt while avoiding a major confrontation with the United States by pushing Cairo toward a negotiated settlement of the dispute with Israel. In the end they were able to achieve neither: they found themselves forced to support Sadat's attack on Israel in October 1973 and then were expelled from Egypt altogether within three years of the conclusion of the war. The experience with Egypt, more than anything else, shaped the Soviet Union's responses to subsequent Third World involvements.

The new set of tactical principles evident in Soviet behavior since the mid-1970s tackled the problem of the quality of Soviet influence by advocating more active interference in the internal affairs of client states. One new tactic was to institutionalize the relationship with the Soviet Union and make it more permanent—that is, no more Sadats.[12] In the process the Soviets could hope to improve the degree of day-to-day cooperation and to increase their control. Other principles included:

☐ In addition to arms transfers, direct military intervention by proxy forces like the Cubans, together with Soviet logistical support and expanded advisory missions;

☐ Establishment of direct police controls over the internal security apparatuses of client regimes, particularly through the efforts of the East Germans;

☐ Efforts to push local leaders to establish "vanguard" parties, and the concomitant centralization of economic and political organs on a Leninist model;

☐ Where the choice was available, greater support for local Communist parties, not out of ideological conviction but because such parties tend to be more reliable politically;

☐ And, finally, the building of a socialist Third World "collective security" network by which different members of the community could protect one another from deviationism in an organized fashion.

Cuba is, in many respects, the lynchpin of this system. Havana's principal function has been to supply combat forces and to relieve the Soviet Union of the need for highly visible direct intervention. Equally important, however, has been its role in initiating those involvements. From the early 1960s, Cuba has been involved sooner and in more countries in the Third World than the Soviets themselves; indeed, through the early 1970s the Cubans engaged in protracted polemics with Moscow over issues like the importance of armed struggle and guerrilla war (the so-called *foco* theory). Although the Cubans in some sense capitulated to the Soviets on the ideological question and muted their criticisms of Soviet caution and conservatism in support of national liberation movements, in practice the USSR was drawn into a number of involvements that might not have occurred had it acted on its own.

Cuba's close alignment with Moscow is based on several factors, the most important of which are Havana's economic dependence on the Soviet subsidy, its reliance on the deterrent effect of Soviet military power against the United States, and Castro's ideological orientation, which puts many of his own interests directly parallel to those of the Soviets. In addition, Cuba's DGI and other security services are well penetrated by Soviet-bloc intelligence. Coordination of Cuban and Soviet activities is by no means total. It is possible to cite any number of instances where the views of Moscow and Havana have diverged. The Cubans were much quicker to recognize the revolutionary potential of the Sandinista movement in Nicaragua than the Soviets, who initially instructed the Nicaraguan Socialist Party (that is, the orthodox local Communist Party) to stand aloof from the Sandinistas. In Angola, Cuban forces actually had to help suppress a coup attempt in May 1977 by Nito Alves, who was reportedly a staunch supporter of close association with Moscow rather than Havana.

But though the Cubans are not robot-like proxies, it is possible to make too much of their divergences with the Soviets.[13] The Cuban "deviation" generally consists of seeing opportunities for action sooner than the Soviets and a willingness to take greater risks on behalf of ideological brethren. In almost all cases, beginning with Angola, the Soviets were eventually convinced to go along with the Cuban game.

The potential of these new tactical innovations is best illustrated by the East Germans, who have played what is perhaps an equally valuable role in terms of Soviet interests. The East German Ministerium für Staatssicherheit (MfS) has helped to organize the internal security organs in Angola, Mozambique, Libya, Ethiopia, the PDRY, Guinea-Bissau, São Tomé, Nicaragua, and a number of other countries (a few of them even turned up in tiny Grenada). Libya's Khadafy has been protected for the past several years by a bodyguard organized by an East German intelligence official named Karl Hanesch, who reportedly saved the Libyan leader from major assassination attempts on at least two occasions in 1978 and 1981.[14] Now Khadafy is far from being a pliant Soviet proxy—he is too much of an adventurist for Bolshevik tastes—but the Soviets are clearly better off with him alive than dead, since Khadafy's Libya has itself been a major player within the socialist collective security system.[15] The East Germans give Moscow a means of actively ensuring that he stays alive, and they are a source of intelligence and influence (Hanesch is also said to be a close personal confidant). Similarly, the East Germans were heavily involved in restructuring the PDRY's security services at the time of the dual assassinations of the presidents of North and South Yemen in June 1978. We do not have direct evidence about the East German involvement in either event, but it would be very surprising if they did not play a role in helping Abd al-Fattah Ismail overthrow Selim Rubai Ali, and they may well have engineered the coup themselves.[16]

The potential significance of direct police controls at the upper echelons of a weak Third World state is evident if one compares the cases of Egypt and South Yemen. When Sadat decided to expel the Soviet advisers in July 1972, Moscow had no choice but to comply with his wishes. Needless to say, the Soviets did not have the capability to project forces into Egypt to prevent the expulsion—as they did in Afghanistan. But neither did they have the less visible option of overthrowing the recalcitrant client by having their own or proxy security advisers aid local rivals for leadership, as apparently happened in the PDRY. The Soviets did try to co-opt Ali Sabri shortly after Nasser's death as an alternative to Sadat, but this amounted to little more than an attempt to manipulate internal Egyptian palace politics rather than exertion of anything that could be called police powers, and in the end they failed miserably. Control over internal security networks in the Third World, as in the case of Eastern Europe in the late 1940s, is a significant qualitative change in Soviet posture and may potentially be more important than any quantity of Cubans or arms transfers.

The establishment of "vanguard" parties, preferably Marxist-Leninist ones, represents a longer term Soviet investment in the institutionalization of their relationship with the client. A vanguard party provides the Soviets with multiple entry points into the client's top leadership and alternatives to the man at the top; helps to ensure some organizational structure that has a chance of surviving the personalized rule characteristic of many Third World states; serves as a kernel from which to build and control other centralized Leninist institutions; and provides a counter to revolutionary spontaneity (for example, the Ethiopian People's Revolutionary Party [EPRP] in Ethiopia). It is desirable that a vanguard party should have a Marxist-Leninist ideology as well. By itself, ideology does not ensure a convergence of interests between patron and client, as the cases of the People's Republic of China, Yugoslavia, and Kampuchea demonstrate. But all other factors being equal, a Marxist-Leninist party will tend to be a more reliable client, as Soviet experience with African, Islamic, and other syncretist forms of Marxism demonstrates.

Hence we find the Soviet Union investing heavily in communist Cuba and Vietnam, establishing multiple ties with an avowedly Marxist regime in Aden, encouraging Angola's ruling Popular Movement for the Liberation of Angola (MPLA) and Mozambique's Front for the Liberation of Mozambique (Frelimo) to transform themselves organizationally into Leninist parties, helping to consolidate the control of the ruling party in the PDRY, and pushing Ethiopia's Mengistu to form a vanguard party, the Commission for Organizing the Party of the Working People of Ethiopia (COWPE). Of course, promotion of local Communists does not always work: in 1977, Communists in the Iraqi army were viciously suppressed by the Ba'athist regime in Baghdad. Clients like Mengistu, moreover, seem to understand the Soviet game and for that reason have deliberately resisted Soviet blandishments to increase COWPE's power.[17] Nonetheless, Moscow's chief clients of the late 1970s differed qualitatively from those of the 1960s in terms of the internal character of their regimes. This in turn had important implications for the Soviet strategic position, since an openly Marxist-Leninist regime will generally have fewer compunctions about open cooperation with the USSR on security matters.[18]

There is evidence to suggest that manifestations of the tactics outlined above are not haphazard occurrences, but represent a systematic approach that has been thought out in advance.[19] Each instance of "cooperative intervention" has manifested more or less the same clear-cut division among the Soviets and their different proxies. Consider, for example, the following description of the laundering operation behind arms supply to the guerrillas in El Salvador:

> particular care was taken to disguise the origins of [Soviet-bloc] military aid. Czechoslovakia offered the Salvadorian guerillas nontraceable Czechoslovak arms, circulating in the world market, to be transported in coordination with East Germany. Bulgaria promised German weapons, "rebuilt from World War II," and East Germany was to donate military training, especially for clandestine operations. Ethiopia offered "several thousand weapons" of Western origin, and Vietnam some 60 tons of U.S.-made rifles, machine guns, mortars, rocket launchers, and ammunition. Nicaragua considered giving Western-manufactured arms in exchange for the communist-made weapons that had been promised the guerillas. Iraq made a $500,000 "logistic donation" for use in Nicaragua and El Salvador.[20]

This account leaves out Libya, whose transports were detained in Brazil in 1983 for ferrying arms to Managua. All of this could have come about spontaneously, of course, reflecting each ally's comparative advantage in the free market of proxy services. But it is possible to multiply examples of Soviet-bloc interventions that required fairly elaborate coordination between different clients, all of which suggests some degree of centralized planning by either Moscow or Havana. In the summer of 1973, Soviet ships were used to transport PDRY troops to support the Dhofar rebellion in Oman. Guinea-Bissau served as a staging base for Cuban planes on their way to Angola in 1976. Soviet planes were used to airlift Soviet and East European equipment and Cuban combat troops to Ethiopia in 1977–1978, using logistics facilities previously established in the PDRY.[21] Conversely, when the president of South Yemen, Selim Rubai Ali, was overthrown by Abd al-Fattah Ismail in 1978, forces loyal to Ismail were supported once again by Cuban troops, ferried by Soviet aircraft— this time from Ethiopia. And in late 1981 Libya, Ethiopia, and South Yemen, with Soviet encouragement, signed a tripartite pact codifying their relationship of mutual support.

Needless to say, the tactical principles I have outlined above do not apply universally to all Soviet Third World clients; several countries in which Moscow has a large stake have remained free of substantial penetration and do not seem to participate actively in the socialist collective security system. Syria, for example, was a major Soviet preoccupation in 1982–1983 and the object of political and military investment on a level not seen in the Middle East since 1970. Despite Assad's eventual signature of a friendship and cooperation treaty in 1980, Syria continues to manifest a prickly independence from Soviet control, as evident in its crushing of the PLO in Lebanon. In spite of the large number of Soviet combat forces manning SA-5 and other sites in Syria, there is little question that Assad could dismiss them as Sadat did; it is Rif'at Assad and not some East German intelligence operative who controls internal security throughout Syria. India, as well, has remained aloof from the Soviets since the Afghan invasion. Indeed, it is difficult to see how a country as large and as independent as India could ever be drawn into the Soviet system, except as a result of an autonomous ideological decision on its part. Generally speaking, the new tactics to make Soviet influence more permanent have a chance of succeeding only in countries without highly developed national traditions or institutions. Precisely those regimes with weak power bases and minimal internal legitimacy are most dependent on Soviet-bloc support and therefore susceptible to penetration and control. Angola, Mozambique, and the PDRY did not even exist as distinct national entities prior to their association with the Soviet bloc, in contrast to older clients like Egypt or Syria. Hence the Soviet client with perhaps the weakest internal position of all, Afghanistan, eventually became the beneficiary of the largest Soviet presence.

Finally, it should be noted that the success of these new tactics is far from assured. Moscow's degree of control over countries within the system varies widely and nowhere approaches the level of influence achieved over its Eastern European allies after World War II. For example, South Yemen is by most criteria the most thoroughly penetrated of the Soviet clients, being a self-avowed Marxist-Leninist state, signatory of a friendship treaty, host to Soviet combat forces, and so on. Yet Marxism remains a thin veneer on the politics of South Yemen; the rivalries within the ruling party in the PDRY remain tribal, regional, and sectarian and may yet lead to an erosion of the Soviet position there.[22] The fact that the new Soviet approach to the Third World may not ultimately work or is not of universal applicability does not make it less of a system, however, and it is still a useful tool for predicting future Soviet behavior.

THE FUTURE

We have seen how Soviet Third World policy has been shaped by the search for positions of concrete geostrategic value, particularly in the 1950s and 1960s, and, in the past decade, by efforts to improve the quality of Moscow's influence with existing or recently acquired clients. What is future Soviet policy likely to be?

The big Soviet push for major new geostrategic positions seems largely finished now, and this factor will be much less important in the rest of this decade. The reason for this lies in the past success of Soviet policy. The U.S.-orchestrated containment barrier was largely broken by the 1960s, partly through Soviet efforts and partly through local developments like the Iraqi revolution, in which Moscow played little role. The Soviets currently have incomparably better access to the oceans and airspace on their periphery than they did in 1955. Similarly, the USSR was able to implement forward naval deployments in the Mediterranean, the Indian Ocean, the southern Pacific, and the Caribbean in the following decade. It is difficult to identify a pressing strategic requirement that will determine the future course of Soviet Third World policy in a parallel fashion.

Of course, this is not to say that the Soviets would not gladly accept a base in the Philippines or Iran if one fell into their laps, nor would they spurn an invitation to return to Somalia or Egypt. The Persian Gulf and Indian Ocean area in particular remains of great strategic significance, and it is a region in which Soviet access and support could stand considerable improvement. The traditional Russian attitude toward security suggests that the Soviets have certain congenital difficulties in deciding when enough is enough. In any event, since Soviet expansionism is largely opportunity-driven, major developments will be dependent on regional stimuli beyond Moscow's control.

The real question, however, is to what degree narrowly defined military interests rather than broad political concerns will shape policy. What price will Moscow be willing to pay to acquire new bases and facilities? As noted above, there is evidence of at least a certain faction within the Soviet leadership that is reluctant to take on costly new obligations in the Third World to clients of dubious staying power and reliability. Since this viewpoint appears to have been associated with Andropov himself, the impact of these views on actual policy may depend on the outcome of the current succession struggle. In any case, we do not see Gorshkov lobbying as energetically or as visibly for access to particular countries as he did in the mid-1960s.

The other issue I have raised, concerning the quality of existing client relationships, does seem to be one with which the Soviets will continue to contend. Particularly if there is a retrenchment in Soviet Third World policy for economic or security-related reasons, the Soviets will have to be concerned with making the best of what they already have. Unlike the acquisition of new clients, moreover, this is one area in which Soviet policy has some room for initiative and creativity. This suggests that in the future we may see something like a bimodal distribution of close Soviet clients: one grouping would consist of states like Vietnam and Syria that are important for their strategic positions, but remain independent and subject to minimal Soviet control, and at the other end of the spectrum would be a cluster of states like Angola and Mozambique, which have lesser strategic value but are more effectively integrated into the Soviet collective security system.

NOTES

1. One conspiracy theory popular in conservative Arab circles in the late 1970s was that Soviet activities in Ethiopia and the PDRY were part of a "pincer movement" aimed at cutting off Western access to Persian Gulf oil. Although this description of the aim is undoubtedly accurate, the Soviets did not exactly choose to end up in those particular countries. Given the choice, it is likely they would trade both for their former position in Egypt.

2. One exception to this general observation may be the April 1978 coup in Afghanistan by which the People's Democratic Party of Afghanistan first came to power; there is some evidence that the Khalq and Parcham factions of the party were brought together at Moscow's instigation in 1977 and perhaps encouraged to seize power. Even so, it is doubtful that the Soviets envisioned the train of events that led to their invasion of the country in December 1979.

3. For example, Khrushchev sent notes to the United States, Britain, and France on September 2, 1957, during the Syrian-Turkish crisis. He proposed negotiations between the four powers on an agreement on the mutual renunciation of force and restraint in arms deliveries.

4. The Soviet sea-based deterrent has also included cruise-missile-firing submarines since the 1950s, with deployment and support requirements similar to early generation SSBNs.

5. See Michael MccGwire, "The Rationale for the Development of Soviet Seapower," *U.S. Naval Institute Proceedings/Naval Review*, May 1980, pp. 165–66.

6. The number and visibility of the surface combatants and long-range Soviet Naval Aviation (SNA) aircraft needed to protect these bastions has increased enormously. The Soviets, however, have evidently deployed a number of Delta-class SSBNs in the mid-Atlantic (that is, outside their normal bastions) as one response to the U.S. deployment of Pershing IIs and ground-launched cruise missiles (GLCMs) in Europe.

7. See MccGwire, "Rationale for Development of Soviet Seapower," pp. 168–69.

8. To my mind, North Yemen is one of the most puzzling of all Soviet aid cases. Moscow poured in the neighborhood of $750 million into this country following the 1979 border confrontation with the PDRY. Although their objective was clearly to prevent North Yemen from falling totally under Saudi influence, the payoff that the Soviets get in return for this enormous investment is very marginal.

9. The Soviet gamble has evidently paid off, since Moscow has been able to replace Berbera with Dahlak Island and Asmara on the Red Sea coast.

10. I am indebted to two Rand colleagues, Alexander Alexiev and Stephen Hosmer, for many of the insights in this section. See Alexander Alexiev, *The New Soviet Strategy*

in the Third World, Note N-1995-AF (Santa Monica: The Rand Corporation, June 1983); and Stephen Hosmer and Thomas Wolfe, *Soviet Policy and Practice Towards Third World Conflicts* (Boston: Lexington Books, 1983).

11. See Francis Fukuyama, *The Soviet Union and Iraq Since 1968*, Note N-1524-AF (Santa Monica: The Rand Corporation, 1980).

12. Although some of these principles, particularly the emphasis on vanguard and/or Communist parties, have been alluded to in Soviet writings, the account below is drawn almost entirely from actual Soviet *behavior* since 1976. Since Brezhnev's death in 1982, there has evidently been a debate on general Soviet Third World policy in Soviet leadership circles, with one group (which apparently included the late Andropov himself) arguing for retrenchment and greater selectivity among Third World clients. The prevalence of such a view would not be at all inconsistent with the interpretation of recent Soviet policy presented here. For evidence of this debate, see Stephen Sestanovich, "Does Moscow Feel Pinched by Third World Adventures," *Washington Post*, May 20, 1984.

13. See, for example, William Durch, "The Cuban Military in Africa and the Middle East: From Algeria to Angola," *Studies in Comparative Communism*, Spring–Summer 1978.

14. *L'Express*, November 4–10, 1983, pp. 104–5.

15. Beyond Africa and the Middle East, the Libyans have been supporting revolutionary groups in Central and South America and as far away as the Philippines.

16. In addition to protecting existing positions, the East Germans have played an active role in creating new ones. There is considerable evidence that they (though not the Cubans) played a major role in training and encouraging the Katangan exile FNLC forces that invaded Zaire's Shaba province in 1978. See Jiri Valenta and Shannon Butler, "East German Security Policy in Africa," in Michael Radu, ed., *Eastern Europe and the Third World: East v. South* (Colorado Springs: Praeger, 1981), pp. 142–45.

17. In other cases, the Soviets have simply guessed wrong about who would be in the vanguard. For example, they discouraged local Communist parties in Central America from forming a united front with noncommunist leftist groups like the Sandinistas prior to the Nicaraguan revolution, a decision they later reversed.

18. Of course, Nasser's bourgeois-nationalist regime in Egypt granted the Soviet navy port privileges, but this was strongly resisted until the disaster of the June 1967 war, when Nasser felt compelled to turn to the Soviet Union for greater military assistance.

19. "Thought out in advance" does not necessarily mean "thought out all at once"; the different elements of this strategy appear to have been developed incrementally, beginning with the intervention in Angola. Moreover, credit for the authorship of these tactics may belong in many cases more to the Cubans than to the Soviets.

20. Quoted in Hosmer and Wolfe, *Soviet Policy and Practice Towards Third World Conflicts*, pp. 102–3.

21. Another example of Soviet-Cuban coordination is the fact that Moscow supplied some 30 pilots to Cuba to replace pilots who had been sent to Ethiopia.

22. For an excellent discussion of internal PDRY politics, see Laurie Mylroie, *Politics and the Soviet Presence in the People's Democratic Republic of Yemen: Internal Vulnerabilities and Regional Challenges*, Note N-2052-AF (Santa Monica: The Rand Corporation, 1984).

Soviet Strategy and Organization: Active Measures and Insurgency

Richard H. Shultz, Jr.

INTRODUCTION

Since the early 1970s, the Kremlin leadership has escalated significantly its role in promoting and assisting various insurgent movements in the developing world. This has been documented in a number of studies.[1] Soviet policy toward the Third World was initially reformulated during the latter half of the 1950s. In the period following Stalin, the Kremlin leaders revealed more of a willingness to send arms and other assistance to "national liberation" movements. Moscow likewise began to actively promote the cause and strategy of these movements in the international arena. With this decision, key elements of the Soviet apparatus expanded their activities in support of this new policy. For example, according to Robert Kitrinos, the International Department of the central committee of the Communist Party of the Soviet Union (CPSU) "expanded its activities into what . . . Khrushchev saw as a new horizon in Soviet foreign relations, namely, the Third World."[2] Similarly, during this period Soviet intelligence was redirected to become a more "flexible, sophisticated, political weapon capable of playing an effective role in support of policy." According to one former Soviet intelligence officer, as a result of this decision "a number of organizational changes were made in the KGB."[3]

Only during the late 1960s and early 1970s, however, as a result of Moscow's perception of a favorable shift in the East-West correlation of forces (the Soviet assessment of the balance of power), did Kremlin leaders apparently decide to expand significantly their involvement with Third World insurgent movements. In order to carry out this new policy, the Soviets escalated their own and their surrogates' political-warfare and military force capabilities.[4] Moscow employs these assets both to promote the cause and strategy of insurgent movements in the international arena and to assist these forces militarily "on the ground."[5]

Various studies have examined how the Soviets employ certain military instruments, particularly arms transfers, to assist guerrilla movements. Very few analysts, however, have paid attention to the role of propaganda and political-influence techniques in this aspect of Soviet strategy and policy. Even more surprising is the absence of any systematic assessment of how Moscow integrates all of these instruments within their overall political-military strategy. Once the decision is taken to assist a particular insurgent movement, available evidence suggests that political and military instruments are synchronized and orchestrated systematically to achieve maximum effectiveness. Policy objectives are attained not by any one instrument, but through the arrangement and simultaneous amplification of all political and military means deemed effective. This is the sine qua non of the Soviet approach.

The purpose of this study is threefold: first, to describe each of these political and military instruments employed by the Soviets and their surrogates for assisting insurgent movements; second, to identify the relevant parts of the Soviet apparatus involved in planning and implementing these techniques; and, third, to use selective examples to highlight how the Kremlin integrates and orchestrates these measures within their overall strategy and policy.

SOVIET POLICY INSTRUMENTS AND ORGANIZATIONAL APPARATUS

The instruments of power and influence utilized by the Kremlin leadership range from propaganda and various political-influence techniques to paramilitary assistance. More specifically, these include:

ACTIVE MEASURES

Political Measures	*Paramilitary Measures*
foreign propaganda	arms and logistical support
international front organizations	political-military training
political activities within international and regional organizations	advisory assistance
	deployment of forces

Apparently, the Soviets now use the term *active measures* to describe many of these political and paramilitary techniques for influencing events and behavior in, and actions of, foreign countries. In terms of support for insurgent movements, both the political and paramilitary elements of active measures are important for achieving policy objectives. Political measures are utilized to champion the cause and objectives of the insurgents in the international arena. International acceptance of the just cause of the insurgency and the "repressive immoral" character of the incumbent regime can play an important role at each stage of insurgent development. Paramilitary assistance, in addition, seeks to improve the political-military proficiency of the insurgents to conduct operations against the target government. What follows is a brief examination of each of these instruments and an identification of those parts of the Soviet apparatus charged with planning and implementing them.

Political Measures

Among the principal Soviet political techniques employed to promote the cause of insurgent movements in the international arena, *foreign propaganda* is of primary importance. Since the period prior to the Bolshevik seizure of power, propaganda has been an important instrument of policy. According to one leading authority, "Lenin established a tradition within which Bolshevik professional revolutionaries and, later, specially trained functionaries of the Soviet state . . . have systematically employed modern communications techniques."[6] Propaganda remains an important instrument for conducting political warfare.

Escalation in propaganda coverage of an insurgent movement often indicates that it has become a more consequential policy issue for Moscow. It also triggers the initiation of a broader political-warfare campaign, in which other political and paramilitary instruments are brought into play (for example, the activation of international front organizations). In the case of the South West African People's Organization (SWAPO), for instance, Soviet overt propaganda set the thematic pattern for the other political-warfare instruments and signaled the amplification of the international campaign.

The Soviet message is transmitted through a vast and coordinated array of propaganda channels, including international broadcasts, numerous publications circulated worldwide, and two major news services.[7] An examination of this output reveals the degree to which Moscow can mobilize and integrate specific propaganda campaigns. They are characterized by the Soviet technique of *kombinatsia*, the combining and integrating of multiple issues in support of a specific policy. In the case of the Soviet propaganda campaign in support of SWAPO, six specific themes (with multiple subthemes) were integrated and combined into a broadly targeted international effort. Other general features include intensity and concentration, flexibility and adaptivity, deception and manipulation, and centralized control and coordination.[8]

Because these campaigns are conducted on an international basis, they can be expected to be broad in scope. This is due, in part, to the fact that multiple audiences are targeted. The Soviet campaign in support of the North Vietnamese and Vietcong is a case in point. The message for Third World states was that Moscow was aligned with and actively supporting the cause of "national liberation." The Kremlin also sought to present an image of the United States as the new neocolonial power. To the Europeans the objective was to characterize the United States as warlike, recklessly aggressive, and capable of plunging Europe into a world war over Vietnam. The call for worldwide opposition to American policy was part of a long-term post–World War II campaign to characterize the United States as the greatest threat to world peace. In light of these multiple objectives, it is not surprising that propaganda campaigns in support of specific insurgent movements are cast so broadly.

What is interesting about the Vietnam case, as well as a number of subsequent ones, is the extent to which the United States is characterized as a major cause of the conflict. The degree or even absence of U.S. involvement appears to have no apparent impact on the way in which Soviet propaganda covers the subject. Consequently, whether the Vietnam War, Namibia, Nicaragua (prior to the Sandinista victory), or El Salvador—four very different cases in terms of U.S. involvement—there was little variance in the Soviet propaganda pattern.[9]

Within the Soviet apparatus, the International Information Department (IID) of the CPSU Central Committee was established in 1978 to improve the coordination of what was already an impressive program of foreign propaganda activities. Not a great deal is known about the IID, and there are conflicting opinions regarding its purpose and scope of responsibilities. Available evidence, however, suggests that it neither sets the propaganda line nor has responsibility for programmatic guidance. These appear to be the duty of the International Department of the CPSU Central Committee (under Politburo direction).[10] The IID, on the other hand, concentrates on improving the coordination of the various overt propaganda channels.

A second political technique for promoting internationally the cause of insurgent movements is through the activities of Soviet-directed *international front organizations*. As with many other aspects of Soviet policy and organization, the use of international fronts can be traced back to the early days of the regime. Lenin saw the importance of advancing Soviet foreign policy objectives through broad organizations that, because of their ostensibly idealistic objectives, would attract greater support than openly Communist parties.[11] The Comintern was assigned responsibility for organizing and directing the fronts, and during the 1920s and 1930s a number of them came into existence.[12]

Soviet overt propaganda themes in support of insurgent movements are promoted and enhanced through the Kremlin's major international fronts. Their techniques include propaganda and international conference diplomacy. The latter is the more action-oriented of the two techniques and can take the following forms:

☐ *Meetings of the front organization.* The fronts use their own deliberations as international forums to promote the cause of different insurgent
movements. Once the meeting is completed, a communiqué is released
and a final report is published (both are used for propaganda purposes).
The representatives of the national-level affiliates of the fronts are then
expected to promote the themes of the meeting back home.

☐ *International and regional conferences sponsored by one or more fronts.*
The fronts will use international and regional conferences, which are
attended by both front and nonfront individuals and organizations, to
promote insurgent causes. These may be either regionally or internationally focused and have, on occasion, run on an annual basis (the World
Peace Council's Stockholm Conference on Vietnam ran from 1967 to
1972).

☐ *International conferences involving the U.N. or regional organizations.*
The major fronts will attempt to link themselves to different U.N. committees and organizations. This includes participating in and even cos-
ponsoring U.N. international and regional conference activity. (This is,
for example, a major focus of front activity in support of SWAPO.) They
also will do this with other nongovernmental and regional organizations,
including the nonaligned movement and the Organization of African
Unity (OAU).

The purpose of each of these techniques is to reach a much larger audience than
the Soviets could hope to influence on their own. In the case of SWAPO, two of
Moscow's major international fronts—the World Peace Council (WPC) and the
Afro-Asian People's Solidarity Organization (AAPSO)—utilized all three conference diplomacy techniques.[13] The escalation in these activities by the WPC
and AAPSO coincided with the activation of other Soviet political-warfare
tactics. The use of fronts in the current campaign to mobilize support for the
guerrillas in El Salvador reveals a different pattern. Rather than one or two
fronts having primary responsibility, a broader and decentralized campaign is
being waged, in which a coalition of a number of fronts is employed. No one
organization appears to have responsibility for conducting the majority of
operations.

Through their various publications the fronts conduct propaganda campaigns in support of insurgent movements. In almost every respect their general
thematic pattern mirrors Soviet commentary. Some differences can be detected,
however. For example, in the case of Central America the number of themes
covered are fewer and the treatment of issues is more simplistic in approach and
vitriolic in tone than that found in Soviet overt propaganda. The front campaign has focused on audiences in the region and has carried a basically simple
message that is played back through international and regional conference

activities. The principal theme concentrates on U.S. policy in Central America in general, and El Salvador in particular. In this and other cases, one can see the difference between the broadly directed front campaigns.

The International Department (I.D.) has responsibility for directing the front organizations as well as conducting relations with nonruling Communist parties. As one specialist points out, however, its duties extend far beyond those publicly identified, and its lineage apparently can be traced back to the Comintern:

> For the formulation of political strategy (including foreign policy) one must look to the Central Committee [of the CPSU] rather than the Ministry of Foreign Affairs. The critical department here is the Central Committee's International Department, headed since the 1950s by Boris Ponomarev. This Department, under various names, dates back to 1943, the year the Comintern was dissolved. Ponomarev was a high official in the latter body, which is viewed by some observers as the lineal predecessor to the International Department.[14]

Schapiro likewise argues that the I.D. is more important than the Ministry of Foreign Affairs: "it seems beyond dispute that the International Department is the element in the Soviet decisionmaking process which gathers information on foreign policy, briefs the Politburo, and thereby exercises, subject to the Politburo, decisive influence on Soviet foreign policy.[15]

In addition to planning and coordinating active measures, as well as implementing them through over a dozen major international fronts and several nonruling Communist parties, John J. Dziak notes that the I.D. "has its own representatives in a number of Soviet embassies under special Central Committee tasking." These include "such sensitive areas as relations with the United States, the Middle East, and West Europe, among others."[16] This has been substantiated by former Soviet officials. For example, Sakharov has noted that Ponomarev's cadres in effect run critical Soviet embassies and orchestrate active measures through Soviet diplomats, the GRU (Chief Intelligence Directorate of the general staff), trade and aid personnel, and even the KGB. Likewise, former KGB officer Stanislav Levchenko, who specialized in active-measures operations, supports this view of the central importance of the I.D.[17]

A third technique increasingly utilized by Moscow since the early 1970s is *political action within the U.N. and other international and regional organizations.* The Kremlin has sought to align itself (and its bloc and surrogate states) with radical and anti-Western Afro-Asian states in these organizations to promote "revolutionary" alternatives in the Third World. Alvin Rubinstein notes that in 1960, when "seventeen new nations—sixteen of them African—became independent and members of the UN," Moscow "seized the moment to propose a declaration . . . embodying the most radical denunciation of colonialism in all its aspects and calling for the independence of all colonial countries and peoples."[18]

By the early 1970s, Soviet cooperation and support for the radical Afro-Asian bloc within the U.N. appears to have paid dividends in various ways. This is the case with respect to the PLO, SWAPO, MPLA, ANC, and other insurgency movements. Increasingly militant, the Afro-Asian bloc has pressed the initiative in the U.N. to support and assist these movements, with the encouragement and direct involvement of the Soviet Union and its surrogates. One important result—among many—has been the granting of permanent observer status to SWAPO, the PLO, and other such groups, and their recognition as the sole legitimate representatives of the people they claim to be fighting for. Additionally, Soviet access to and support from Third World states and movements has been enhanced.

In sum, the Soviet Union approaches the U.N. and other international and regional organizations, according to Rubinstein, as arenas of political warfare:

> Conflict, not cooperation, is the dynamic that impels Soviet behavior in international organizations . . . the USSR has taken to bloc politics in the UN with a vengeance, exploiting voting majorities to weaken the West and advance Soviet proposals and preferred resolutions. International organizations are battlefields for competing ideas and approaches to concrete issues, and Moscow has decided the game is worth the effort.[19]

This appears to be true of Soviet promotion of SWAPO and other similar movements. Moscow uses the U.N. as a forum to promote insurgent causes and to enhance their reputations and credibility.

Of the three political-warfare instruments examined in this paper, this seems to be the most difficult for Moscow to employ. In large part, this is due to the environment in which Moscow and its surrogates have to operate. These are not controlled situations, and this will affect the degree to which the Kremlin can successfully employ political-influence techniques. For example, during the latter half of the 1960s, before the U.N. power balance shifted to the anti-Western stance of the 1970s, Moscow sought to maneuver the General Assembly to take up the question of U.S. involvement in Vietnam. The Soviets were unsuccessful in this effort. In addition to the unfavorable power balance that existed at that time, there was no specialized committee concerned with Vietnam through which Moscow could lay the foundation for such action within the General Assembly.

By the 1970s, Soviet fortunes in the U.N. changed. Consequently, they were able to be more effective in promoting certain insurgent movements. This is evident, for instance, in the SWAPO and PLO cases. Specialized U.N.

committees exist and Moscow and its surrogates have been actively involved in their deliberations.[20] As these committees became increasingly militant, U.N. support and assistance to SWAPO and the PLO increased significantly. Through an alliance with likeminded Afro-Asian states, the Soviets and their surrogates have been increasingly able to promote the cause of "liberation" movements in the U.N.

In the case of Central America, the U.N. appears to be of secondary importance. This is probably due to the fact that no specialized committee structure exists through which to promote the cause of guerrilla movements in this region. As a result, it appears that, beginning in 1979, Moscow chose to use its Cuban surrogate to maneuver the nonaligned movement toward more active support for insurgent movements in Central America. Soviet strategy seeks to use all avenues for building international support for these groups. As the head of the nonaligned nations in 1979, Cuba was instrumental in focusing their attention on this subject.

Although specific components of the organizational apparatus involved in conducting specific active-measures techniques have been identified above, others are more difficult to ascertain. This is true of political action within international organizations. Existing evidence does suggest a large KGB and bloc intelligence role in the U.N. In 1983, R. Jean Gray, head of the FBI's New York section, estimated that there are 1100 communist-bloc officials in New York, including 150 Soviets in the U.N. missions and about 180 in the Secretariat. Arkadi Shevchenko, a former official of the Soviet Ministry of Foreign Affairs who served as under-secretary general of the United Nations from 1973 to 1978, estimates that 30 percent of Soviet U.N. employees, including those in the missions and the Secretariat, are skilled KGB officers.[21] Others believe that 40 or 50 percent of all Soviet and bloc officials in the United States are intelligence officers. They further suggest that one-half of these are what the Soviets term "line-PR" officers. These officers have responsibility for political matters, including overt and covert collection of information and active measures (each will have responsibility for one to five agents of influence).[22] If we use Gray's figure of 1100 Soviet-bloc officials in New York and estimate that 40 percent are intelligence, we arrive at a figure of 550. One-half of these would be line-PR, conducting active measures in the U.N. and elsewhere. In Moscow, Service A, located within the KGB's First Chief Directorate, has responsibility for planning and overseeing these covert active measures.[23]

The I.D. also is involved in political active measures in the U.N. First of all, several Soviet-controlled international front groups (for example, the World Peace Council), which are officially recognized as nongoverning organizations (NGO), take part in U.N. deliberations. Since the fronts are under the direction of the I.D., these organizations can be employed for influence operations. Whether the I.D. has officials in the Soviet U.N. mission, similar to its representation in key embassies in the United States and Western Europe, is uncertain. Some believe that, given the importance of the active-measures effort in the U.N., the I.D. is likely to have its own representatives in place. Others suggest that although the I.D. plans and coordinates active measures, its officials are not operationally involved at the U.N.

Paramilitary Measures

Although international propaganda and political action aim to establish insurgent legitimacy in the world arena, the objective of Soviet paramilitary assistance is to improve insurgent operational effectiveness on the ground. Since the early 1970s, significant growth in this form of assistance has coincided with the expansion of the political instruments described above. The principal kinds of paramilitary assistance include arms and logistical support, political-military training of insurgent cadres, and advisory assistance.

The military establishment and the Committee for State Security (KGB) are among the key elements of the Soviet apparatus for implementing these activities. With respect to the military, since the early 1970s authoritative sources have identified a much greater external role for the Soviet armed forces. In fact, as early as 1968, Marshal Sokolovskiy stated that the USSR "will render, when it is necessary, military support" to "national liberation" movements.[24] In 1974, writing in a leading party theoretical journal, *Problems of History of the CPSU*, Marshal Grechko, then minister of defense, explained that the responsibilities of the Soviet armed forces were now to be extended into entirely new areas:

> At the present stage the historic function of the Soviet Armed Forces is not restricted to their function in defending our Motherland and the other socialist states. In its foreign policy activity the Soviet state purposefully opposes the export of counterrevolution and the policy of oppression, supports the national liberation struggle, and resolutely resists imperialist aggression in whatever distant region of our planet it may appear.[25]

Since the mid-1970s this theme has been articulated frequently in Soviet military writing. The paramilitary techniques identified above are implemented through specific directorates of the Soviet military's General Staff and the KGB.

The importance of *arms and logistical support* to insurgent movements is readily apparent. It is essential to their growth and development.[26] A detailed analysis of the various insurgent movements receiving arms and the different channels through which the Soviets transfer them is not, however, possible relying solely on open sources. In certain cases there is little doubt where and how the arms arrive, whereas in other instances the evidence is quite fragmentary, and Moscow seeks to maintain a policy of nonattribution. To accomplish this, the Soviets use covert and indirect channels, especially via surrogates and Third World states. This is, for example, true in the case of SWAPO. Since the latter half of the 1970s, arms have been transferred through the front-line states. According to one source, beginning in the latter half of the 1970s, this military assistance included "T-34 and T-54 tanks, 122 millimeter rocket launchers, personnel carriers, and large quantities of small arms. Much of the equipment was landed in Dar es Salaam, Tanzania, and Maputo and Beria, Mozambique."[27] More recently, Soviet and bloc military equipment has been transmitted to SWAPO through Angola.

A similar pattern can be observed in Central America. During preparation for the final FSLN offensive in Nicaragua in 1979, arms from Bulgaria, East Germany, Hungary, and Czechoslovakia were shipped to Cuba, flown from Cuba to Panama, transshipped to Costa Rica on small planes, and supplied to guerrillas based in northern Costa Rica. An analogous situation exists with respect to the Salvadoran insurgents. Although Cuba provides few of its own weapons, it plays a key role in coordinating the acquisition and delivery of arms from Vietnam, Ethiopia, and Eastern Europe through Nicaragua. The arms flow continues through a clandestine air and surface network directed by Havana.

The Military Assistance Directorate of the general staff appears to have principal responsibility for directing Soviet and surrogate arms transfers and other forms of logistical support. In addition to the transport of equipment, personnel from the Military Assistance Directorate can be found playing a support role in Third World states contiguous to the location of the insurgency conflicts.[28] It should be noted that the GRU utilizes staff members of the Military Assistance Directorate in Third World countries for cover. This allows them to conduct espionage and penetration operations in country, as well as to provide assistance to insurgent groups.

Beyond arms and logistical support, Moscow and its surrogates provide *political-military training for insurgent cadres.* There are, however, important analytic distinctions to be noted. First, training is not confined to military tactics, but also entails political-ideological techniques. This includes, for example, instruction in how to establish an insurgent infrastructure. Second, political-military training can take place within the USSR or one of its surrogate states, as well as in base areas contiguous to the actual location of internal conflict. Training will vary according to whether the insurgency is in an initial or more advanced stage. Finally, the level of support will depend on the degree to which the Kremlin believes the insurgency can contribute to its foreign policy objectives.

In the USSR a network of facilities has been established for basic and advanced training of insurgent and terrorist cadres. Perhaps the best known of these are the Lenin Institute and Patrice Lumumba University. Each provides instruction in military and political-warfare tactics. Additionally, the Soviets maintain more specialized facilities for advanced training, including those at Simferopol in the Crimea, and near Odessa, Tashkent, and Baku.[29] In the *KGB Today*, John Barron identifies a special KGB complex near Moscow known as Balashikha. Under the supervision of the First Chief Directorate's Department 8 of Directorate S, Barron explains, "a school in one area of the grounds provides training in terrorism to students imported directly from Third World countries or from Patrice Lumumba University in Moscow."[30] Additionally, more specialized training may take place at the military and higher military schools and academies of the Soviet armed forces. This may be true particularly of schools for "special designation" (*spetsnaznacheniia* or *spetsnaz*) units. These troops are charged by the CPSU with missions too sensitive for the regular military. The border guard schools at Alma-Ata (named for Dzerzhinskii), Golitsyno (named for Voroshilov), and Moscow (named for Mossovet) are one possibility.[31] Ministry of Internal Affairs (MVD) schools also may be used for advanced training.

Training of insurgents and terrorists can take place in Soviet-bloc and surrogate facilities. In 1980 Cuba helped Salvadoran guerrillas contact Arab radical states and movements to arrange military training. Also at this time Havana sharply increased its own training of a guerrilla army capable of mounting a major offensive against the Salvadoran military. According to one source, groups up to battalion size are under instruction, and selected elements receive more intensive training on specialized subjects.[32]

Although information is sketchy on specific parts of the apparat involved in training insurgents in both the USSR and surrogate facilities, elements from the general staff's Chief Intelligence Directorate (GRU) and the KGB apparently play key roles. These elements fall within the "special designation" or *spetsnaz* category noted above.

Paramilitary training in irregular or special tactics is not a new phenomenon for the USSR. The origins of this facet of active measures, as with political dimensions, can be traced back to the early days of party rule. During World War II, the Central Committee of the CPSU established a Central Staff of the Partisan Movement, which conducted guerrilla operations behind German lines.[33] According to Dziak:

> Apparently three groups exercised strong influence over the partisan movement: the General Staff's Chief Intelligence Directorate (GRU), the Fourth Directorate of the NKGB, and the Armed Forces Counterintelligence Directorate (GUKR, NKO, or SMERSH) headed by General Abakumov, an NKGB officer. The two former of these three were part of the state security apparatus. SMERSH, though nominally subordinate to the Commissariat for Defense, was in fact directly answerable to Stalin.

Dziak goes on to observe that "the Partisan experience had a profound impact on subsequent Soviet planning and organization for special operations." After World War II "spetsnaz units gradually took on external roles," including the training of insurgent and terrorist cadres.[34]

As noted above, within the KGB's First Chief Directorate, Department 8 of Directorate S is involved in insurgent and terrorist training. It probably maintains links with training facilities in Third World countries.[35] The Cubans, East Germans, Bulgarians, and other surrogates also are involved in guerrilla training, under KGB guidance. In addition to Department 8, this may involve Department 11 of the First Chief Directorate, which conducts liaison with and penetrates the intelligence services of Soviet satellite states. Other KGB elements that might be involved in insurgent and terrorist training are the border guards and the troops of the Ninth Directorate.[36] These links between *spetsnaz* forces and training facilities both inside and outside of the USSR are difficult to establish.

KGB officers are complemented by their GRU counterparts, who likewise provide expertise in guerrilla, diversionary, and intelligence training to Third World insurgents and terrorists. As with the KGB, specific elements within the GRU play roles in the agency's intelligence training and insurgency branches.

Finally, documentation indicates that military aid personnel from the general staff's Military Assistance Directorate are present in large numbers throughout the developing world. They likely assist KGB and GRU officials in conducting training.

In sum, Dziak explains that the Soviets (and their surrogates) maintain large numbers of elite or quasi-elite forces tasked with missions clearly political-military in nature. This includes the use of KGB, GRU, and general staff elements to train insurgent cadres both inside and outside the USSR.[37]

For analytic purposes, we have distinguished training from *advisory support*. In terms of the Soviet apparatus, this distinction may not be meaningful. Many of the military and security organs involved in training also provide advisory support. Important distinctions, however, can be drawn in terms of function and location. First of all, advisory assistance generally appears to take place in areas contiguous to the location of the insurgency. For example, within sub-Saharan Africa, Soviet and surrogate officials provide advisory support to SWAPO guerrillas in base areas in Angola and Zambia. Functionally, this includes tactical intelligence, irregular combat direction, and other forms of on the ground paramilitary advisory support.

Surrogate Assets

Imperial regimes have frequently used others to project power and to gain influence beyond their borders. In early times, for instance, the Romans made the *clientes* fight various enemies. More recently, the British used Gurkhas in Malaya, and the French have relied on the Foreign Legion. The Soviet use of surrogates, however, differs in many respects from these examples. Soviet surrogates are much more specialized in the missions they perform; Soviet control appears to vary markedly; and proxies play a political-military role in peace as well as in war.

Although specialists have written about Soviet proxies, confusion persists over both the nature of the patron-client relationship and the mission specialization of the surrogates. With regard to the former, it would seem inaccurate to categorize these relationships as uniform. Moscow's control and influence appears to vary. In terms of certain clients there is little divergence of opinion about the nature of the relationship. In other cases there is significant disagreement.

The Soviet–East European bloc association is the least contentious for Western specialists. The patron has the power and expects obedience from the client in all missions. Trond Gilberg has characterized these states as "faithful agents," who consider "themselves as representatives of the Soviet Union in the Third World." Their activities are "designed to enhance the stature of the Kremlin and its power and influence . . . in ideological, political, and military-strategic terms." The East Germans, Czechs, and Bulgarians belong in this category. In the cases of Poland and Hungary, Gilberg perceives a difference. Although they remain "true to the principle of solidarity with the Soviet Union," he detects "less enthusiasm than [is] the case among the 'faithful agents.'"[38] Although an interesting thesis in light of the fact that the Soviets rely on East Germany, Czechoslovakia, and Bulgaria, Gilberg does not document his assertion.

Perhaps the most debated patron-client relationship is that of Moscow and Havana.[39] On the one hand, there are those who believe that Havana is not performing as a Soviet proxy in Africa or elsewhere, but follows a foreign policy linked directly to the early days of revolutionary rule in Cuba. According to Edward Gonzalez, Cuban policy is the result of the wranglings between three elite factions—pragmatists (technocrats and managers), *fidelista* (revolutionary anti-imperialists), and military professionals (advocates of an offensive military role in support of foreign policy objectives).[40] Cuba's policy in Africa is the result of the victory of the latter two factions. Thus, though Cuban and Soviet policies converge, Havana is self-motivated and is not following Moscow's directions.

Gavriel Ra'anan, on the other hand, marshals evidence pointing to Cuba playing a surrogate role on behalf of the Soviet Union: "To guarantee Cuba's economic, and perhaps military, viability and to insure implementation . . . of the 'Brezhnev Doctrine,' Castro would have to cooperate and even closely collaborate, with the USSR . . . by 1973, Castro had already committed himself to the USSR, not only in terms of trade, but also ideologically." Ra'anan, however, goes on to observe that in addition to much-needed economic assistance, playing a surrogate role provides Castro with "an opportunity to reassert the regime's virility... Consequently, the Cuban venture in Africa, starting in Angola, constituted the natural confluence and culmination of three factors": ideological predilections, Castro's need to bolster the fading image of the regime, and the phenomenon of increased Soviet-Cuban cooperation based on complementary needs and capabilities.[41] Beyond economic dependence, which is considerable, other analysts believe that Moscow maintains influence over Havana through penetration of Cuban security services, particularly the DGI.[42]

In sum, the case of Cuba is a difficult one. Laqueur has framed the dilemma in terms of a question—is Cuba's role to be understood as a paladin or surrogate? In light of the evidence, it seems highly unlikely that Cuba is acting independently. We would concur with Laqueur: "despite outward appearances, Cuba no more has a specific African policy than Bulgaria does."[43]

Whereas Soviet-Cuban relations have been the subject of extensive Western scrutiny, other communist surrogate states have received little attention. For example, what kind of influence does Moscow maintain over the North Koreans and Vietnamese, and can we expect them to play increased surrogate roles in the future? Similar questions should be raised about Marxist-Leninist governments in Angola, Ethiopia, Nicaragua, and South Yemen. Finally, what about cases like Libya under Khadafy? Clearly, he has helped promote the aims of Soviet foreign policy (for example, Libyan assistance to guerrillas in Central America and elsewhere). It would seem inappropriate, however, to place Libya in the surrogate category. Another difficult case to differentiate is that of the PLO. This is due both to its factional composition and to its changing power base.

If we need to know more about the nature of Soviet-surrogate power relations and how Moscow influences and/or controls its proxies, analytical efforts also should be directed toward sharpening our understanding of the functional tasks or specialization of Soviet surrogates. For example, in southern Africa the East Germans and Cubans serve various functions. Chester Crocker, assistant secretary of state for African affairs, has characterized this as a "communist division of labor."[44] According to two specialists, "the security mission of the East Germans in Africa has been broadly defined... there are about 2500 East Germans training the Angolan army and the Namibian insurgents, the South West African People's Organization (SWAPO)." Evidently, East German troops stationed in Angola also have "participated in search and destroy missions against the UNITA insurgents and challenged the spearhead of South African columns deep inside Angola in November 1981." In addition to training, advising, and limited combat support, during postinsurgency periods of power consolidation the East Germans provide sophisticated knowledge of the military and intelligence sciences. In Angola, a core of advisers are training the regime's intelligence and security services.[45]

Cuba likewise plays multiple roles in southern Africa and elsewhere in the developing world. In Africa this has involved political-military training of both insurgent and government forces, as well as actual combat involvement. Because of Cuba's "Third World credentials," they have a great deal of credibility among states and movements in these regions. As a result, this provides Havana with the potential for achieving long-term penetration, leverage, and control on behalf of its Soviet patron.

In terms of political techniques, Cuban and East German personnel are active in the front organizations and promote insurgent movements through political action in the U.N. and other international organizations (for example, the Cuban role in the nonaligned movement). Their overt propaganda is also targeted to support these efforts. Other Soviet clients play similar roles in supplementing Moscow's propaganda and political efforts in support of insurgent movements.

In addition to Cuba and the German Democratic Republic, one can observe the involvement of other Soviet surrogates in southern Africa. For example, the Bulgarians have provided military assistance to African liberation movements, including the MPLA in Angola, SWAPO in Namibia, and the Patriotic Front in Zimbabwe. Similarly, accounts of the weaponry used by Third World insurgent movements reveal that Czech arms constitute an important part of their arsenal.[46]

In sum, a wide range of surrogate political and military assets supplements and enhances Soviet capabilities for assisting insurgent movements both internationally and on the ground. Here we have focused on surrogate involvement in southern Africa. This pattern has been followed in Central America and elsewhere, benefiting Moscow in a number of ways. In the first place, surrogate assets expand an already impressive array of Soviet capabilities. These allow the Kremlin to acquire more flexible means for implementing policy. The use of surrogates also permits plausible denial in those situations in which Moscow does not wish to reveal its role.

Coordination and Integration

During the last ten to fifteen years, Soviet strategy for assisting "revolutionary" insurgent movements has evolved not only in terms of the range and sophistication of political-military instruments employed but also with regard to their coordination and integration. This is reflected, for example, in Soviet support for SWAPO. In the aftermath of Angola, Moscow escalated its assistance to SWAPO. This new policy was set forth officially by the Kremlin in

1978 with the publication of a "Manifesto for the Freedom, Independence, National Revival, and Social Progress of the Peoples of Tropical and Southern Africa."[47]

Increased support actually began in 1976–1977. The political-military instruments described above were activated and synchronized almost simultaneously. Thus, as Soviet overt propaganda escalated to promote the cause of SWAPO, the same themes were advanced by the Kremlin's major international front organizations. Through propaganda and conference diplomacy, the WPC and AAPSO significantly intensified their efforts. Similarly, in the U.N. and other international organizations, Moscow and its surrogates and fronts stepped up their political activities to bolster and legitimize SWAPO.

Political techniques are part of an integrated Soviet political-military strategy. Consequently, the paramilitary elements of active measures were intensified simultaneously with propaganda and other political-influence techniques to assist SWAPO operationally on the ground. This coordination of multiple Soviet instruments was augmented by surrogate assets.

CONCLUSION

Moscow employs a number of political and military instruments to assist guerrilla movements. Use of these instruments is not a recent development. As stressed above, there is a historical continuity in their application that dates back to the early years of communist rule in Russia. Although not called active measures at the time, the various political and military techniques described in this paper were employed by Lenin and those who followed him to achieve foreign policy objectives.

What is different since the early 1970s is the degree to which these techniques have been integrated, orchestrated, and implemented to promote and assist Third World insurgent movements. As Soviet policy shifted to one of increasing activism in the developing world, its political-military strategy required new supports for this involvement.

In light of the above, can we expect these trends to continue in the years ahead? Given the growth of organizational and financial assets and the highly integrated political-military strategy that has evolved, to say nothing of the successes Moscow has achieved, it would seem unlikely that the Soviets will lessen their efforts. Beyond the issue of degree of involvement, it is possible that Moscow will add new variations in its use of these political and military instruments. This may be especially true of its employment of surrogate capabilities. There would appear to be room for further innovation and diversification. Recently, however, the USSR has had to devote more attention to assisting newly established Marxist-Leninist regimes in the Third World to consolidate power. These states, which include Afghanistan, Angola, Nicaragua, and Ethiopia, are facing anti-Communist movements. This directing of resources to assist in "power consolidation" may result in less support for certain insurgent movements.[48] Nevertheless, it would seem likely that in the years ahead Moscow will follow a dual policy of helping insurgent movements seize power and assisting those who succeed to consolidate control.[49]

NOTES

1. Richard H. Shultz, Jr., "The Role of External Forces in Third World Conflicts," *Comparative Strategy* (Fall 1984), pp. 79–111; Walter Laqueur, *The Pattern of Soviet Conduct in the Third World* (New York: Praeger, 1983); Stephen Hosmer and Thomas Wolfe, *Soviet Policy and Practice Toward Third World Conflict* (Lexington, Mass.: Lexington Books, 1983); Robert Donaldson, ed., *The Soviet Union in the Third World: Successes and Failures* (Boulder, Colo.: Westview Press, 1981).

2. Robert Kitrinos, "International Department of the CPSU," *Problems of Communism* (September–October 1984), pp. 49–50.

3. Anatoliy Golitsyn, *New Lies For Old* (New York: Dodd, Mead, 1984), pp. 47, 49.

4. Stephen Kaplan, ed., *Diplomacy of Power* (Washington, D.C.: Brookings Institution, 1981), chaps. 2–5; Mark Katz, *The Third World in Soviet Military Thought* (Baltimore, Md.: Johns Hopkins University Press, 1982); Gavriel Ra'anan, "Surrogate Forces and Power Projection," in Uri Ra'anan, Robert Pfaltzgraff, and Geoffrey Kemp, *Projection of Power* (Hamden, Conn.: Archon Books, 1982), pp. 283–333.

5. Shultz, "The Role of External Forces in Third World Conflict."

6. Frederick Barghoorn, *Soviet Foreign Propaganda* (Princeton, N.J.: Princeton University Press, 1964), pp. 4–5.

7. Richard H. Shultz, Jr., and Roy Godson, *Dezinformatsia: Active Measures in Soviet Strategy* (New York: Pergamon-Brassey, 1984), chaps. 2–3.

8. Ibid.

9. Richard H. Shultz, Jr., "A Study of Soviet Propaganda and Political Support for Third World Insurgencies" (unpublished manuscript).

10. Shultz and Godson, *Dezinformatsia*, pp. 25–31.

11. The general purposes of the front organizations appear to be as follows. First, they enable Moscow to promote its policy (under the camouflage of peace, racial equality, national liberation, and so on) to a much wider audience. They also provide a means for criticizing and isolating the Soviet Union's main enemies strategically, politically, and morally. Fronts offer a way to improve the image of the Soviet Union internationally by distracting attention from repressive and aggressive Soviet policies. The fronts focus on the real and alleged shortcomings of Soviet enemies, while remaining silent on Soviet problems. They also defend aggressive Soviet foreign policy like the invasion of Afghanistan. Finally, the fronts may assist the KGB in spotting targets for recruitment. For background on the fronts, see Witold Sworakowski, *The*

Communist International and Its Front Organizations (Stanford: Hoover Institution on War, Revolution and Peace, 1965); James Atkinson, *The Politics of Struggle* (Chicago: Regnery, 1966); John Roche, *The History and Impact of Marxist-Leninist Organizational Theory* (Cambridge, Mass.: Institute for Foreign Policy Analysis, 1984); Roy Godson, *Labor in Soviet Global Strategy* (New York: National Strategy Information Center, 1984).

12. See Gunther Nollau, *International Communism and World Revolution: History and Methods* (New York: Praeger, 1961); Franz Borkenau, *World Communism* (reprint, Ann Arbor, Mich.: University of Michigan Press, 1962).

13. The concept of conference diplomacy is borrowed from Arieh Eilan, "Conference Diplomacy," *The Washington Quarterly* (Autumn 1981), pp. 24–29. See Shultz, "A Study of Soviet Propaganda and Political Support for Third World Insurgency."

14. John J. Dziak, *Soviet Perception of Military Power: The Interaction of Theory and Practice* (New York: National Strategy Information Center, 1981), p. 40.

15. Leonard Schapiro, "The International Department of the CPSU: Key to Soviet Policy," *International Journal* (Winter 1976–77), p. 44.

16. Dziak, *Soviet Perception of Military Power*, pp. 40–41.

17. Vladimir Sakharov and Umberto Tosi, *High Treason* (New York: G. P. Putnam's Sons, 1980). For a background sketch on Boris Ponomarev see "The Foreign Departments of the Central Committee of the CPSU," *Radio Liberty Research Bulletin* (October 27, 1980), pp. 14–18, 21–24. See also Shultz and Godson, *Dezinformatsia*, chap. 5.

18. Arieh Eilan, "Soviet Diplomacy in the Third World," in *The Pattern of Soviet Conduct in the Third World*, chap. 2; Alvin Rubinstein, *Soviet Foreign Policy Since World War II* (Cambridge, Mass.: Winthrop, 1981), p. 196, chaps. 9–10.

19. Ibid., pp. 210, 212.

20. For example, in the case of SWAPO, the key U.N. body Moscow has concentrated on is the Committee of 24 (or, Special Committee on the Situation with Regard to the Implementation of the Declaration on the Granting of Independence to Colonial Countries and Peoples). In the case of the PLO, it has been a much more diversified approach. See Juliana Pilon, "The United Nations' Campaign Against Israel," *Backgrounder* (June 16, 1983).

21. See 1983 Appropriation Request of the FBI before the House Subcommittee on Appropriations, April 1, 1982. Also cited in Juliana Pilon, "The UN and the USSR," *Survey* (Autumn–Winter 1983), pp. 95–96.

22. Based on interviews conducted with former senior U.S. intelligence officials, as well as former Soviet and bloc intelligence and diplomatic officials.

23. See Shultz and Godson, *Dezinformatsia*, pp. 31–33.

24. V. D. Sokolovskiy, *Soviet Military Strategy*, ed. and trans. by Harriet Fast Scott (New York: Crane Russak and Co., 1975), pp. 180–84.

25. A. A. Grechko, "The Leading Role of the CPSU in Building the Army of a Developed Socialist Society," *Problems of History of the CPSU* (May 1974). Translated by *FBIS* (May 1974). Cited in Harriet Scott and William Scott, *The Armed Forces of the*

USSR (Boulder, Colo.: Westview, 1979), p. 57. For current excerpts of official Soviet military commentary, as well as analysis of these developments, see: Harriet Fast Scott and William Scott, eds., *The Soviet Art of War* (Boulder, Colo.: Westview, 1982); and Mark Katz, *The Third World in Soviet Military Thought* (Baltimore, Md.: The Johns Hopkins University Press, 1982).

26. Larger amounts of arms become especially important as the insurgency reaches its more advanced (what Shackley terms the "operational") phase of conflict. At this point, the opposition is able to "surface to confront security forces in open combat. Their tactics are now more hit than run." During earlier phases, few arms are required because violent tactics are confined to sabotage and terrorism. See Theodore Shackley, *The Third Option* (New York: McGraw-Hill, 1981), p. 87.

27. Daniel Papp, "The Soviet Union and Southern Africa," in Donaldson, *The Soviet Union and the Third World*, p. 79. Also see Peter Vanneman and Martin James, *Soviet Foreign Policy in Southern Africa* (Pretoria: Africa Institute of South Africa, 1982).

28. For a discussion of the development of Soviet power projection capabilities in the 1970s, see W. Scott Thompson, *Power Projection* (New York: National Strategy Information Center, 1978); more recent developments are described in Hosmer and Wolfe, *Soviet Policy and Practice Toward Third World Conflict*; and in Kaplan, *Diplomacy of Power*.

29. Neil Livingstone, "Terrorism: The International Connection," *Army* (December 1980), p. 16.

30. John Barron, *KGB Today* (New York: Reader's Digest Press, 1983), p. 21.

31. Harriet Fast Scott and William Scott, *The Armed Forces of the USSR* (Boulder, Colo.: Westview, 1979), chap. 11. See also Vladimir Kuzichkin's piece in *Time*, November 22, 1982, pp. 33–34, where he specifically identifies a terrorist training school at Balashikha.

32. *Cuba's Renewed Support for Violence in Latin America*, Special Report no. 90 (Washington, D.C.: United States Department of State, 1981), p. 7.

33. See John J. Dziak, "Soviet Intelligence and Security Services in the 1980s: The Paramilitary Dimension," in Roy Godson, ed., *Intelligence Requirements for the 1980s: Counterintelligence* (New York: National Strategy Information Center, 1981), chap. 4. Dziak notes that Yuri Andropov served with the partisans during World War II. Although Andropov is recognized for expanding the KGB's role in political active-measures campaigns directed against the West, this suggests that he was also inclined toward the paramilitary techniques under discussion. Ibid., p. 110.

34. Ibid., pp. 96, 99–100.

35. See John Barron, *KGB: Secret World of Secret Agents* (New York: Reader's Digest Press, 1974); Leonard Schapiro, "The Soviet Union and the PLO," *Survey* (Summer 1977–78); Claire Sterling, *The Terror Network* (New York: Holt, Rhinehart, Winston, 1981); U.S. Congress, Senate, Subcommittee on Security and Terrorism of the Committee on the Judiciary, *Terrorism: The Role of Moscow and Its Subcontractors*, 97th Congress, 1st sess. (Washington, D.C.: GPO, 1981).

36. Brian Crozier, *The Surrogate Forces of the Soviet Union*, Conflict Studies no. 92

(London: Institute for the Study of Conflict, 1978); and Barron, *KGB Today*, appendix B, "Organization of the KGB."

37. Dziak, "Soviet Intelligence and Security Services in the 1980s."

38. Trond Gilberg, "Eastern European Military Assistance to the Third World," in John Copper and Daniel Papp, eds., *Communist Nations' Military Assistance* (Boulder, Colo.: Westview, 1983), pp. 74–75.

39. See Rose Gottemoeller, "The Potential for Conflict Between Soviet and Cuban Policies in the Third World," *Conflict*, no. 4 (1984), pp. 245–65.

40. Edward Gonzalez, "Complexities of Cuban Foreign Policy," *Problems of Communism* (November–December 1977), pp. 3–9.

41. Ra'anan, "Surrogate Forces and Power Projection," pp. 298–99.

42. Barron, *KGB: Secret World of Secret Agents*; Crozier, *The Surrogate Forces of the Soviet Union*; and Robert Leiken, *Soviet Strategy in Latin America*, Washington Papers (New York: Praeger, 1982).

43. Laqueur, *The Pattern of Soviet Conduct in the Third World*, p. 15.

44. U.S. Congress, Senate, Subcommittee on Security and Terrorism of the Committee on the Judiciary, *Soviet, East German, Cuban Involvement in Fomenting Terrorism in Southern Africa*, vol. 2, 97th Congress, 2d sess. (Washington, D.C.: GPO, 1982), p. 26.

45. Vanneman and James, *Soviet Foreign Policy in Southern Africa*, pp. 38–39; and Ra'anan, "Surrogate Forces and Power Projection."

46. Gilberg, "East European Military Assistance to the Third World," pp. 81–82.

47. For the text, see *The African Communist* (London), no. 75, fourth quarter, 1978.

48. Francis Fukuyama, "Gorbachev and the Third World," *Foreign Affairs* (Spring 1986).

49. Richard H. Schultz, Jr., "Soviet War of Surrogates to Project Power into the Third World," *Parameters: Journal of the Army War College* (forthcoming, Fall 1986).

PART II

Cuba: First Among Equals

Mark Falcoff

Although the precise relationship between Cuba and the Soviet Union since 1959 has been the source of considerable debate and controversy, few can deny that the advent of the Castro regime has been one of the three or four most important events in the history of Soviet foreign policy. For one thing, unlike the puppet governments of East Germany, Poland, or the Baltic countries, the Castro dictatorship came about not by force of arms but by "voluntary" adscription; in this sense it could be said that Cuba alone, of all the states in the Soviet community of nations, is a genuinely dependable ally. For another, the acquisition of a Spanish-speaking client state—an opportunity lost with the collapse of the Second Spanish Republic in 1939—has opened vast new cultural horizons to the Soviet Union; in some ways, it amounts to the linguistic equivalent of the acquisition of a warm-weather port. At the same time, the fact that most Spanish-speaking states lie to the south of the United States, and maintain with it a relationship at times heavily charged with acrimony, envy, and resentment, has allowed the Soviets to introduce their own agendas under the disguise of a purely local irredentism. For another—and on a more practical level—the Cuban regime has acted as an important adjunct of Soviet political, diplomatic, propaganda, and intelligence activities in Latin America. It has also functioned as an active Soviet proxy in far-off theaters of war (Angola, Ethiopia), and as the principal broker of like-minded political forces and governments in the Caribbean region with Moscow.[1] In addition, Fidel Castro himself has actively worked to push the "nonaligned" movement into "anti-imperialist" (that is, pro-Soviet) channels. Moreover, for 25 years the Soviet Union has incrementally developed a military position on the island, "strengthening the image of Soviet power in an overall East-West context, reinforcing the impression of a Soviet counterweight to the United States in Latin America," and—what is perhaps most important—"potentially providing a physical capacity for Soviet access to other areas of the continent as well as to the United States."[2]

THEORIES OF REVOLUTION: CONFLICT AND CONVERGENCE

Prior to 1959, Soviet commentators regarded Latin America as a "semi-feudal" region inevitably consigned to the U.S. sphere of influence. This perception was amply reflected in the actual conduct of Communist parties throughout the region, which was far from revolutionary. Typically, in each country the Communists labored to build broad fronts with "progressive" elements of the so-called national bourgeoisie, laying the presumptive groundwork for a confrontation with this same class at some later ("higher") stage of economic and social development.[3] Operating from so primitive a base of social theory, these parties were ill-equipped to deal with many of the developments in postwar Latin America, and in some countries they paid very dearly for their ignorance. For example, in Chile, having supported the election of President Gabriel González Videla (1946–1952), the Communists found themselves promptly outlawed and driven underground, and in Argentina and Bolivia—two countries that could arguably be regarded as having experienced something akin to a social revolution in the 1950s—they found themselves firmly on the side of the counterrevolutionaries. At the same time, however, in countries like Mexico, Venezuela, Guatemala (before 1954), and even in Cuba itself, the popular-front strategy paid rich dividends in terms of influence in the labor movement, education, and the media, and in the development of full-blown parties with professionally trained bureaucracies. Without taking this fact into account, one simply cannot appreciate the impact of the Cuban Revolution on Soviet thinking and on the ambivalent attitude of entrenched Communist leaders throughout the hemisphere who were, perforce, required to rethink their strategies.

By their actions, and later by the explicit theories drawn to rationalize them, the Cubans challenged the two assumptions on which Soviet thinking about Latin America had rested.[4] First, Castro and his confederates had apparently demonstrated that the "objective conditions" for revolution were already present in all Latin American countries and that such tactical alliances as had been forged with noncommunist parties, movements, and governments were unnecessary if not counterproductive. And, second, Castro's success in defeating a U.S.-backed expeditionary force of Cuban exiles convinced the Soviets to abandon the "geographical fatalism" that had historically consigned the entire region to a position of extreme marginality in their strategic planning.

Since 1959 serious differences have arisen between Moscow and Havana over the degree to which the Cuban experience is immediately applicable to other Latin American countries and, also, what risks are worth running with the United States. But the increasing Soviet commitment to the Cuban regime—in arms, credits, and strategic raw materials—strongly suggests that Moscow is in the Caribbean region to stay. There is really no other way to explain the transfer of resources that, according to the most conservative estimates, amounted in the early 1980s to some $3 billion a year, approximately 25 percent of Cuba's Gross Domestic Product and five times the present level of U.S. aid to all Latin American nations combined.[5] It requires no specialized knowledge of the current state of the Soviet economy to conclude that these contributions to the Castro regime are far from gratuitous.

What these figures indicate above all is a growing convergence between Cuban and Soviet policies in the region and, to an increasing degree, between Cuban and Soviet perceptions of the situation in Latin America. During the 1960s, Castro's insistence on sponsoring guerrilla warfare in countries such as Venezuela, Colombia, Brazil, Argentina, and Peru (with whom the Soviets maintained or wished to maintain normal state-to-state relations) nearly broke the Cuban-Soviet alliance. But judicious application of Soviet economic pressure in 1967–1968, combined with the signal failure of Cuban-sponsored insurgencies on the ground, eventually brought Castro around; in 1968 he endorsed the Soviet occupation of Czechoslovakia and the Brezhnev Doctrine, which among other things asserts the right of the Soviet Union to define the limits of permissible behavior for communist countries.

Since the mid-1970s, the center of theoretical gravity has moved somewhat back in the Cubans' direction. First, their role as proxy forces for the Soviets in Africa underlined their uniquely practical value on Third World battlefields and as such increased Castro's leverage, both ideological and political, with the Kremlin. Second, the success of the Nicaraguan revolution in 1979, the New Jewel coup in Grenada, and the spectacular growth of the FDR-FMLN in El Salvador during 1979–1980 all suggested that the Cuban perception of revolutionary opportunities in the Caribbean Basin was far more accurate than the Soviets had been inclined to think. Meanwhile, a shift in the international posture (or posturing) of a number of Latin American states within the context of the nonaligned movement gave Castro sufficient ideological cover to establish correct diplomatic relations with a number of countries, including those which in the past he had characterized as dominated by "oligarchical" governments—Venezuela, Colombia, Ecuador, Argentina, and Costa Rica. By 1980 the gap between the Soviets and the Cubans on matters of Latin American policy had, for all practical purposes, been closed.

Differences nonetheless remain. Cuba's objective in the Caribbean Basin and, indeed, in Latin America as a whole, is the creation of regimes in its own image and likeness. Castro sees himself as a latter-day Bolívar, destined to liberate the continent from North American "domination"—indeed, obligated to do so, not only to justify his own revolution but to prevent any alternative from reaching the kind of fruition that would challenge his fundamental assumptions. No doubt he would pursue this policy in any case; however, in the absence of Soviet assistance, it would constitute little threat to the United States or to Cuba's neighbors. The Soviets have a more cold-blooded attitude toward the region: although they would welcome the emergence of Leninist regimes, they would be satisfied with far less. For the moment their purposes would be served equally by "progressive" anti-American governments to whom no important commitments need be made, but who would offer the Soviets opportunities to legitimize their naval, maritime, and (what amounts to the same thing) intelligence presence in the area.[6] At the same time, such regimes could be used to distract the United States from concerns elsewhere, opening, in effect, a "second front" in what they like to call America's "strategic rear."[7]

It is important not to exaggerate the practical significance of these differences. A long and sterile debate on whether Cuba is a Soviet "puppet" or "pawn," or whether it acts in a wholly independent manner, has already consumed far more scholarly energies than it deserves.[8] The important point to grasp is that in the short and possibly middle term, Cuban and Soviet objectives are fully coherent, even if—as in El Salvador—Castro's efforts prove less than successful. One could even argue that within Central America, at least, conflict rather than its definitive resolution best serves Soviet interests, since the victory of revolutionary forces would presumably confront Moscow with some hard decisions on the deployment of increasingly scarce resources.

CUBAN-SOVIET MILITARY LINKAGES

Since 1960 the Soviet Union has donated more than $2.5 billion in arms to Cuba, much of it since 1975, when Moscow undertook to support a major modernization of all branches of Castro's armed forces. The effect of this program has been to transform a fundamentally defensive body into one with significant offensive capability, increasing airborne-trained forces to between three and four thousand troops and improving the Cuban army's airlift and sealift capability. Moreover, between January 1981 and late 1984, Soviet merchant ships delivered some 66,000 tons of military equipment to Cuba, roughly five times the *annual* average for the previous ten years. Some have chosen to rationalize this as a response to fear of invasion following the election of a conservative Republican administration in the United States, but it is more easily understood in terms of a new five-year program for upgrading and replacement of exhausted stocks, which was already on the boards at the time of

President Reagan's first inauguration. Nor can this development be separated from Cuba's active support for the new revolutionary regime in Nicaragua or the insurgency in El Salvador: substantial portions of materiél from these shipments are meant to replace items—particularly small arms and ammunition—already shipped to Central America.

The Cuban army is the largest in the Caribbean Basin and the second largest in Latin America (after Brazil, a country that possesses roughly ten times its population). At this point it is also the only Latin American military institution to have participated in overseas combat since World War II, giving both its army and air force personnel recent experience in operating many of the sophisticated weapons in their inventory. In particular, the Cuban air force is one of the largest and probably the best equipped in Latin America, boasting some 200 MiGs and two squadrons of Floggers; the MiG-23s have a capacity to operate throughout the Caribbean Basin, so that in Nicaragua, for example, they could be employed in either a ground-attack or air-superiority role. They could have played a similar role in Grenada following the completion of the 9,000-foot runway there, had not the regime of Maurice Bishop come to an end in late 1983.[9]

The armed forces are among the most reliably pro-Soviet elements in the Cuban power structure. Armed Forces Minister Raúl Castro, the dictator's brother, has long been known as "Moscow's man" in Havana, and his views are reinforced by an entire cadre of officers who are graduates of the M. V. Frunze Military Academy in the Soviet Union. As of 1972, some 275 Cubans had successfully completed training at this institution, and at this writing they hold most of the important posts in the military and administrative structure. This includes missile and radar bases, which are under their absolute control. It is not uncommon for the graduates of an elite military institution such as West Point to dominate an armed forces establishment; what is remarkable in the Cuban case is the degree to which those trained abroad have come to constitute a political class all their own. Unique, too, is the interpenetration of party and army. As Irving Louis Horowitz, arguably the leading student of the subject, has written, not even the Soviet Union has "so close an identification of party and military. Raúl [Castro] himself has provided the one hundred percent isomorphism between Communist party activities and Cuban military activities of the officer corps."[10]

The Soviet military presence in Cuba is not limited to proxies. At present it includes a ground-forces brigade of 2,600 men, comprised of one tank and three motorized rifle battalions as well as various combat support units. The Soviets have also stationed on the island a military advisory group of 2,000, an intelligence-collection facility—the largest outside the USSR—and a complement of six to eight thousand civilian advisers and technicians. The combat brigade represents a symbolic commitment to Castro—implying a readiness to defend Cuba if invaded and also presumptively raising for the United States the diplomatic and strategic costs of such a course. In all likelihood it provides security for Soviet personnel and key Soviet facilities, particularly the intelligence-gathering unit. And, in the event of a power struggle within the Cuban leadership, the brigade is there to ensure the victory of the pro-Soviet faction, should the possibility of international realignment (or even neutralism) ever arise.[11] The military advisory group provides technical advice and training with sophisticated weaponry, particularly MiGs, surface-to-air missiles, and Foxtrot submarines; some members are attached to Cuban ground units. The intelligence unit monitors U.S. military and civilian communications.

Cuba has also been the site of an extensive naval visitation program. Some 21 Soviet naval task groups have been deployed to the Caribbean since 1961, virtually all of them visiting Cuban ports. The most recent visit (April–May 1981) included for the first time a Kara-class cruiser, the largest Soviet combat vessel ever to have visited the island. In addition, Soviet intelligence-collection ships operating off the eastern coast of the United States call there, as do hydrographic research and space-support ships operating in the region. Since 1975, Soviet TU-95 Bear D reconnaissance aircraft have been deployed periodically to Cuba, generally during times of international tension or during U.S., NATO, or Soviet exercises. In addition, the Soviets have apparently seconded a considerable number of their pilots to augment the island's air defense during periods such as 1976 and 1978, when Cuban pilots were posted to Angola and Ethiopia. This allowed the Cuban air force to operate abroad without diminishing its capacity to fulfill its primary mission.

CUBAN CONTRIBUTIONS TO SOVIET EXPANSIONISM: METHODOLOGIES

During the early 1960s, the Cubans' insistence on full replication elsewhere in Latin America of their own experience in the Sierra Maestra—the *foco* theory of a peasant-based guerrilla insurgency—provoked serious tensions with the Soviet Union, divided the regime from the urban-based Latin American Communist parties, led to the island's expulsion from the organized community of American states, and, most important of all, contributed to the collapse of movements Cuba sponsored in Venezuela, Peru, Argentina, and Bolivia. Since the late 1970s, however, the Cubans have devised a far more sophisticated approach to armed struggle. First, the distinction between urban and rural bases has been abolished; the Cubans have finally come to understand their own revolution (which, in spite of assiduously cultivated myths, was never exclusively rural)[12] and the explosive potential of Latin American cities, which are characterized by a plethora of adolescents of school-leaving age with quite literally nothing to do. Second, the Cubans have discarded the rigid ideological sectarianism that hindered their earliest efforts to export revolution; their front organizations have learned to incorporate a variety of non-Marxist, Catholic, and independent leftist groups without relinquishing control to them. Third, and most important, they have devised a strategy of unification that has finally overcome the chief obstacle to the growth of Latin American Marxist movements—the tendency to splinter and divide along personalist and/or ideological grounds.

The strategy of unification is a gradual one, which may vary slightly according to circumstances. Its main lines are reasonably clear, however.[13] Havana first allies itself to those parties and movements within the target country most nearly in tune with its (and Moscow's) ideological goals. Quite often such groups have already received Cuban training and equipment. Other formations or organizations are persuaded to come aboard (and to subordinate their leadership to a unified command, typically styled a "directorate") in exchange for an assured flow of arms, training, and intelligence, as well as access to an international "solidarity" network that reaches deep into Western countries.[14] In Nicaragua, the pole around which the Cubans chose to arrange their efforts was the Frente Sandinista de Liberación Nacional (FSLN); in El Salvador, the focus was the local Communist party (PCES), the Armed Forces of National Resistance (FARN), and the Popular Liberation Forces (FPL).

To date, the most successful application of this strategy has been in Nicaragua. Though the FSLN had a long history of opposing the Somoza regime, it was but one of many such organizations, and by no means the most numerous or broadly representative. Given its discipline, unity of purpose, and ready access to foreign assistance, however, it was well situated to take advantage of the divisions among genuinely democratic forces. After a final breakdown of dialogue between the opposition and the dictatorship in 1978, the FSLN was able to achieve hegemony within the forces of the opposition. Of critical importance, too, was the care the Sandinistas took to hide their ties to Cuba and the Soviet Union, as well as their Marxist-Leninist ideological commitments.[15] Even after victory, the Sandinistas chose to mask the degree to which unification amounted to manipulation until complete control of the country could be established through a new army, police, and domestic surveillance apparatus. The intent was also to secure as much financial aid as possible from the United States and Western countries.[16]

The same tactics were used under slightly different circumstances in El Salvador in 1979–1980. There a democratic revolution had already overthrown the dictatorship of General Carlos Humberto Romero but had failed to consolidate itself against forces of the extreme left and right. While the provisional government struggled to achieve some mastery of the forces of order and to enact sweeping social and economic changes in the face of considerable public resistance, the four main armed formations of the Salvadoran left met in Havana in May 1980. There, in exchange for (and as a precondition to) Cuban aid, these groups consolidated into a Unified Revolutionary Directorate (DRU). Later, a unified political and propaganda front (the Democratic Revolutionary Front [FDR]) was established, with formal links to the Socialist International, to make the directorate's case for aid from Western Europe and to neutralize attempts by the Reagan administration to counter its challenge on the ground in El Salvador. Though a carefully planned "general offensive" by guerrilla forces in early 1981 failed to achieve its objective, for most of 1982 and 1983 the fate of El Salvador hung in the balance at the U.S. Capitol, where FDR operatives, allies, and sympathizers came within a hair of achieving their objective—a cut-off of U.S. military assistance to the beleaguered Salvadoran government.[17]

Central to the strategy of unification is deception—that is, the techniques used to successfully deny the ideological goals and external links of a revolutionary directorate. This is critical not only to disarm foreign opinion but to achieve what appears to be a genuine coalition between Marxist and non-Marxist elements in the target country. In the case of Nicaragua, for example, the critical moment in Sandinista fortunes came when firmly anti-Marxist elements of the opposition (including leaders of the business community) were finally persuaded to join them in 1979; this convinced many doubters to abandon Somoza, including a number of Latin American countries and, finally, the United States. Deception also allows the Soviet Union to maintain an apparent aloofness from developments in target countries, since the Cubans are willing to play a more active and visible role.[18] It also allows the Soviets to refuse to discuss Central American issues in the context of generalized East-West negotiations.[19]

CUBAN CONTRIBUTIONS TO SOVIET EXPANSIONISM: RESOURCES

Institutional capabilities.   In 1974 the Americas Department of the Cuban Communist Party was given full responsibility for the overall direction of unification strategies.[20] Its director, Manuel Piñeiro Losada, is a former chief of Cuban intelligence and one of the most important party functionaries on the island. He is charged with coordinating the efforts of a wide range of agencies, including the armed forces, the intelligence services (DGI), and the Ministry of Interior (Minint), as well as various supporting elements. Representatives of the department are well placed in Cuban embassies abroad, particularly in the Caribbean, where they sometimes serve as ambassadors or chargés d'affaires. They also serve overseas as employees of the Cuban news agency, Prensa Latina, or Cubana Airlines.

Within Cuba itself, a network of guerrilla camps, including the party's Narciso López Training School, offers instruction on guerrilla warfare, propaganda, and agitation to prospective revolutionaries. The military curriculum includes sabotage, explosives, military tactics, and weapons use. Since 1979, several hundred trainees at a time have come from El Salvador, Nicaragua, Guatemala, Costa Rica, Honduras, Colombia, Grenada, the Dominican Republic, and elsewhere in Latin America. The Cubans also operate training schools for their own nationals—carefully selected intelligence personnel selected for clandestine operations in Latin America, Africa, and the Middle East; here the instructors are not merely Cuban but Soviet, East German, and Czech. Other selected groups are trained in Libya and some of the Eastern European countries.

Greater manpower and trained resources. One of the curious paradoxes of the Cuban Revolution has been its overproduction of technicians and professionals who cannot be absorbed into the local economy, whose absorptive capacities have actually decreased since 1959.[21] The old regime's inability to resolve this contradiction—in the view of some observers—is what imparted a peculiarly radical flavor to Castro's movement once in power.[22] In contrast, the present Cuban government deals with unemployment and underemployment by exporting skilled laborers and technicians to Third World countries, an imperative that has grown all the more acute as the proportion of young adults in the population has reached very significant levels. In Africa, for instance, in addition to combat troops, there are tens of thousands of Cuban civilians operating as economic functionaries, administrative and political technicians, public health officials, teachers, and doctors. Some six thousand of the latter work in Nicaragua alongside the estimated three thousand military and security personnel Castro has dispatched to that country. In Grenada, prior to the fall of the Bishop regime, some eight hundred Cuban construction workers were on the island helping to build, among other things, a new international airport, and another hundred Cuban technicians were in Suriname before their expulsion in October 1983.

Greater logistic capabilities. Cuba still lacks sufficient transport aircraft capable of supporting long-range, large-scale troop movements, and it would have to turn to the Soviets—as in Cuba's African involvements—to achieve such capability. As noted above, within the Caribbean Castro has sufficient aircraft to transport large numbers of troops and supplies. Particularly important in this connection is the recent acquisition of A-26 short-range transports. These planes are capable of air-dropping troops in portions of Florida and Belize, Haiti, Barbados, and the Dominican Republic. If based in Nicaragua, the AN-26s could reach all of Central America in either a transport or air-drop role. In addition, more than thirty smaller military and civilian transport planes, including those used in Angola, could be employed to fly troops and munitions to neighboring countries.

Increased Soviet and bloc cooperation. The most important recent development in Cuban and Soviet overseas activities, particularly in the Caribbean Basin, has been the orchestration of bloc support for revolutionary movements and regimes. Thus, following the arrival of the first high-level Nicaraguan delegation to the USSR and the establishment of party-to-party relations with the CPSU, the FSLN concluded similar accords with East Germany, Bulgaria, and Czechoslovakia. Shortly after that, East German police and intelligence advisers showed up in Nicaragua alongside their Cuban and Soviet counterparts. Likewise, after a party-to-party agreement was reached between the CPSU and the victorious New Jewel Movement in Grenada, similar accords were reached with East Germany, Bulgaria, and North Korea. The captured documents of Grenada indicate that if concrete economic assistance from this quarter was extremely meager, some $40 million in assorted munitions, military equipment, uniforms, and training materials was in the process of being delivered to the Bishop government from the Soviet Union, Cuba, and North Korea.

Access to other global resources. The Cubans have acted in some ways as a broker between the Soviet Union and its allies on the one hand, and revolutionary forces and governments in the Caribbean Basin on the other. Captured documents assembled with the State Department white paper, as well as those uncovered in Grenada, show how Havana provided entrées for the Salvadoran FMLN-FDR in bloc embassies in Mexico City, the Soviet Union itself, and from there to Vietnam, Ethiopia, Libya, and other covert sources of assistance.[23] The Cubans were also of critical importance in orienting Grenadians in the labyrinthine world of international organizations, particularly the Socialist International.[24] In Nicaragua, Libya has extended economic assistance and supplied Managua with military equipment, and the Palestine Liberation Organization (PLO), which provided "volunteers" to fight in Sandinista ranks during the civil war, has provided pilots and mechanics for the Nicaraguan air force.

CUBA'S ROLE: THE CASE OF NICARAGUA

Though many countries contributed to the overthrow of Nicaraguan dictator Anastasio Somoza in 1979, the Cubans undoubtedly maintained the closest relationship with the FSLN. It was Havana that forged the critical unity agreement among the various leftist factions (much as Castro was to do later in the case of El Salvador) and provided the arms that tipped the military balance in the final months. Once the new regime was installed, Cuban diplomats, intelligence agents, military officers, and assorted political operatives assumed a major role in the consolidation of power. According to Miguel Bolaños

Hunter, a former counterintelligence officer for the Sandinista regime, the present director of Nicaraguan intelligence is actually a Cuban who uses the nom de guerre of Renán Montero. Under his apparent direction both Cuban and Soviet operatives function in something approaching a tandem relationship. "In the counter-intelligence unit where I worked," Bolaños stated, "there are two Soviets and a Cuban advisor. There can be at least seven to ten Cubans at any given time; the Soviets only come occasionally to review and brief the F-2 section," that is, the division responsible for surveillance of foreign embassies. In the same document he reported that some seventy Soviet advisers were involved in all aspects of Nicaraguan state security, along with four hundred Cubans (as well as forty to fifty East Germans and twenty to twenty-five Bulgarians). The entire structure of the new security system, including methodology, has been lifted almost without alteration from Cuban and Bulgarian handbooks, and the Soviets have already built a school for state security in Nicaragua.[25]

The Cuban presence is most apparent, however, in the military establishment. There are some three thousand Cuban soldiers (not counting high-level advisers) presently in Nicaragua, plus a covert team of some two thousand soldiers who work as technical advisers, build roads, and handle heavy machinery. Much of this effort is aimed at training recruits for the new army, as well as developing all aspects of army security and defense. The Cubans are also instructing the Nicaraguan soldiers in the use of a plethora of Soviet weapons that Havana and Moscow have unloaded on Managua since 1979, including bazookas, machine guns, mines, and handguns, as well as Katsuka rocket launchers and .45 caliber recoilless rifles, one hundred Soviet tanks, armored transport vehicles, artillery, and heat-seeking SAM-7 missiles.[26]

The primary Cuban impact on Nicaragua is, of course, political. Between the two regimes there is, as Antonio Jorge has written, "a noticeable convergence in ideological persuasion, structures, modus operandi, and even in intangibles such as political and revolutionary style," so that in the end an "intense political-ideology affinity and shared *Weltanschauung* will finally impose itself."[27] Cuba represents the successful transition of a Hispanic-American country from a client state of the United States to a similar relationship with the Soviet Union, a consummation that from many points of view is the desideratum of the Nicaraguan leadership. That this imposes a special role on Cuban advisers in Managua is not, therefore, to be wondered at.

CUBA'S ROLE: THE CASE OF GRENADA

The capture of a huge cache of documents relating to the rule of the New Jewel Movement in Grenada has permitted an even more authoritative evaluation of the Cuban role as the "revolutionary" praxis in the Caribbean.[28] These illustrate that the Cubans were active in setting up parallel organizations to compete with established trade unions, farmers' associations, youth and women's groups; in military training; in providing access to international organizations and the nonaligned movement; as a funnel for economic and military aid from the Soviet bloc; and, most important of all, as a critical source of guidance in dealings with the Soviet Union.

Of particular importance was the role played by the Cubans as an advocate for the Grenadians in the highest circles in Moscow. From the lengthy reports sent back by W. Richard Jacobs, Maurice Bishop's ambassador in the Soviet Union, it is clear that the Soviets were reluctant to make commitments to Grenada beyond their power to fulfill them and had only responded, he wrote, "because Cuba has strongly championed our cause."[29] Grenada's relationship to Cuba was thus roughly congruent to Castro's with the Soviet Union— indicative of a kind of subcontracting of Soviet influence in certain areas of the Third World, where Moscow lacks experience, knowledge, and geographical proximity but possesses a reliable surrogate.

CUBA'S ROLE: NONREVOLUTIONARY STATES

The most "autonomous" aspects of Cuban foreign policy—those that do not appear to respond, at least immediately, to Soviet influence or interests—are apparent in Castro's relations with Caribbean governments that by no stretch of the imagination could be regarded as revolutionary. Probably the best example is Michael Manley's Jamaica (1976–1980), where the socialist aspects of the regime were more apparent in rhetoric and international posturing than in substance, and where the Cuban presence was apparent largely in economic and technical assistance projects (agriculture, tourism, sports, and so forth). A similar policy was followed with Forbes Burham's Guyana, where the links were principally commercial (agreements to purchase rice, lumber, and other goods in exchange for trained Cuban personnel to assist health and education programs). Both Jamaica and Guyana illustrate two aspects of this policy: first, Cuba's tendency to sacrifice the interests of local Communist parties that have little chance of coming to power in order to break out of diplomatic isolation in the region; and, second, the tendency to allow foreign policy to be guided by a curious zero-sum notion of Cuban-U.S. relationships. As Jorge notes, in this region, the Cubans are prepared to do business with any regime that declares itself to be anti-American, "informed by the principle that any net loss inflicted on the United States automatically constitutes a gain for Cuba." What Castro seeks to do, he adds, "is to multiply the geographical loci of confrontations with the United States in the hopes of creating new allies and simultaneously debilitating its main adversary."[30]

FUTURE PROSPECTS

It seems highly unlikely that at any point in the foreseeable future the Cuban regime will redefine its international mission in terms different from, or incompatible with, the Soviet Union. This is true not only for simple reasons of economic necessity but also because Castro and his associates are highly ideological and call upon Marxism-Leninism to explain and justify the entire course of Cuban history since 1959. To question their relationship with the Soviet Union is tantamount to questioning the Cuban Revolution itself, since the only concrete accomplishment Castro can point to over twenty-five years is international realignment. Whether his successors (as even he must, someday, pass from the scene) will choose to define their nation's destiny in these terms remains to be seen, and whether they will be free to act on their changed perceptions is equally unknown.

For the Soviet Union, the special relationship with Cuba does impose serious and weighty obligations of an economic nature, but if twenty-five years and $4 billion have not caused the Soviets to rethink their priorities, it is difficult to imagine under what circumstances this might occur in the future. A more interesting question is the degree to which the Soviets might be willing to assume a similar obligation with respect to Nicaragua or some other client state on the Latin American landmass. In the past, those who wished to minimize the security threat represented by Marxist regimes insisted that the Soviets could not afford "another Cuba"; perhaps, indeed, they cannot, at least on the conventional terms known to bourgeois bankers. Yet their willingness to provide 45 percent of Nicaragua's petroleum (representing an annual extension of some $250 million in credit) does raise some nagging questions about how Moscow goes about making cost-benefit analyses. Moreover, to the degree to which Western countries can be persuaded to subsidize such regimes, Soviet resources are less thinly stretched. This may explain why, among other things, Castro purportedly advised the Sandinistas after their victory not to alienate the United States, and why he so fulsomely challenged Washington to provide the new revolutionary government with large amounts of economic aid.

No doubt for the United States Cuba is a bigger problem than the Soviet Union in Latin America, particularly in the Caribbean Basin. This is so because public perceptions of the Soviet threat generally are well developed in the United States; the Cuban threat, less so. To comprehend the way in which the Soviets develop and use proxy assets requires a greater degree of sophistication than most ordinary citizens can take the time to develop, even if they are careful readers of the quality press. And, of course, the fact that the Cubans genuinely wish to do what they are doing creates an aura of independence and even quasi-legitimacy for their actions. This, combined with Castro's repeated offers to American journalists to settle his differences with the United States (claims that, however, discount from the very start any serious consideration of the outstanding foreign policy and security issues that divide us), imparts a continuing element of confusion to the discussion of U.S. Cuban policy.

NOTES

1. Mark Falcoff, "Bishop's Cuba, Castro's Grenada: Notes Toward an Inner History," in Jiri Valenta and Herbert Ellison, eds., *Soviet and Cuban Strategy After Grenada* (Boulder, Colo.: Westview Press, 1986).

2. Morris Rothenberg, "Latin America in Soviet Eyes," *Problems of Communism* 32, no. 5 (September–October 1983): 1–18.

3. Rollie Poppino, *International Communism in Latin America: A History of the Movement, 1917–1963* (New York: Free Press, 1964), pp. 129–48.

4. Of course, these theories were not fully descriptive of the events themselves. Wrapped in a mythological mantle, they proved a poor guide for others in the late 1960s. See Luigi Einaudi, "Changing Concepts of the Cuban Revolution," Rand Corporation Paper, 1966.

5. Jiri Valenta and Virginia Valenta, "Soviet Strategies and Policies in the Caribbean Basin," in Howard J. Wiarda, ed., *Rift and Revolution: The Central American Imbroglio* (Washington, D.C.: American Enterprise Institute, 1984), p. 213.

6. Ibid., pp. 204–11.

7. R. Bruce McColm, "Central America and the Caribbean: The Larger Scenario," *Strategic Review* 11, no. 3 (Summer 1983): 28–42.

8. The best summary of different views is Robert A. Pastor, "Cuba and the Soviet Union: Does Cuba Act Alone?" in Barry B. Levine, ed., *The New Cuban Presence in the Caribbean* (Boulder, Colo.: Westview Press, 1983).

9. *Cuban Armed Forces and the Soviet Military Presence* (U.S. Department of State, Bureau of Public Affairs), Special Report no. 103 (Washington, D.C., August 1982).

10. "Military Origins and Outcomes of the Cuban Revolution," *Armed Forces and Society* 1, no. 4 (August 1975) and 3, no. 3 (May 1977). See also Marta San Martín and Ramón E. Bonachea, "The Military Dimension of the Cuban Revolution," in Irving Louis Horowitz, ed., *Cuban Communism*, 5th ed. (New Brunswick, N.J.: Transaction Books, 1984).

11. Doubtless the Soviets have learned from their experiences in Egypt and Peru, where no such force was present to protect their investment.

12. Einadi, "Changing Concepts of the Cuban Revolution."

13. "Cuba's 'Strategy of Unification' at Work," in *Western Hemisphere Security: The*

Latin American Connection (Pittsburgh, Pa.: World Affairs Council of Pittsburgh, 1983), pp. 95–112.

14. For some notion of how the Soviets assist such groups internationally, see the document book released with the State Department white paper, *Communist Interference in El Salvador* (U.S. Department of State), Special Report no. 80 (Washington, D.C., February 23, 1981). Of particular interest also is the diary of a trip through the United States by Salvadoran communist functionary Shafik Handal, described in Mark Falcoff, "Central America as a U.S. Domestic Issue," in Wiarda, *Rift and Revolution*, pp. 369–70.

15. A recent study establishes beyond reasonable doubt that at no point did the Sandinistas seriously consider abandoning their ideology or modifying it in meaningful ways—they only adopted methods to disguise its fundamental nature. See David Nolan, *The Ideology of the Sandinistas and the Nicaraguan Revolution* (Coral Gables, Fla.: Institute of Inter-American Studies, University of Miami, 1984).

16. These developments led to a massive defection of many leaders whose organizations had been "unified." This was predictable. Less predictable (and also less easy to explain) was the persistence of Western aid in the face of patent betrayal of the Sandinistas' earlier declared principles.

17. Falcoff, "Central America as a U.S. Domestic Issue," pp. 360–63.

18. "Cuba's 'Strategy of Unification' at Work."

19. Robert Hunter, "Strategy for Central America," in *U.S. Policy in Central America: Consultant Papers for the Kissinger Commission*, special issue of the *AEI Foreign Policy and Defense Review 5*, no. 1 (1984): 61–70.

20. Edward González, "The Cuban and Soviet Challenge in the Caribbean Basin," *Orbis* (Spring, 1985), pp. 73–94.

21. International Bank for Reconstruction and Development, *World Development Report, 1981* (Washington, D.C., 1981).

22. James O'Connor, *The Origins of Socialism in Cuba* (Ithaca, N.Y.: Cornell University Press, 1970).

23. *Communist Interference in El Salvador.*

24. Falcoff, "Bishop's Cuba, Castro's Grenada."

25. "Inside Communist Nicaragua: The Miguel Bolaños Transcripts," Heritage Foundation *Backgrounder*, no. 294 (September 30, 1983).

26. Ibid.; and Morris Rothenberg, "The Soviets and Central America," in Robert S. Leiken, ed., *Central America: Anatomy of Conflict* (New York: Pergamon Press for the Carnegie Endowment, 1984), pp. 131–49.

27. Antonio Jorge, "How Exportable Is the Cuban Model? Culture Contact in a Modern Context," in Levine, *The New Cuban Presence in the Caribbean*, pp. 211–33.

28. The most useful version is Paul Seabury and Walter A. McDougall, *The Grenada Papers* (San Francisco, Calif.: Institute for Contemporary Studies/ICS Press, 1985).

29. "Grenada-Soviet Relations: A Summary, 7/11/83," in ibid., pp. 196–216.

30. Jorge, "How Exportable Is the Cuban Model?" p. 212.

Soviet Proxy Assets in Central America and the Caribbean

Michael S. Radu

The presence of Soviet proxies in the western hemisphere—particularly since the Cuban Revolution and even more spectacularly since the late 1970s—has raised the prospect of communism in the Americas as a permanent and spreading phenomenon. The scholarly literature abounds with claims that the Americas are or should be insulated from the conflict between the superpowers. "Containment, bipolarity, macrolinkage—all suggest that there is a compelling Cold War logic behind U.S. Caribbean policy. But when examined critically, the argument lacks substance. To believe otherwise and behave accordingly is absurd."[1]

The same approach, characterizing most of the U.S. traditional political establishment, was translated into official policy by the Carter administration. It found succinct expression in the report of the Inter-American Dialogue group, which included such personalities as Cyrus Vance, Edmund Muskie, David Rockefeller, General David Jones, and Robert McNamara:

> We all favor keeping Latin America and the Caribbean out of the East-West conflict to the greatest extent possible. It does not serve that purpose for the United States to oppose changes in the region simply because they diminish U.S. influence and hence are perceived as advantageous to Cuba and the Soviet Union, unless they are clearly related to basic security concerns. We believe that the United States can better achieve its long-term interest in regional stability, one shared by Latin Americans, by exercising measured restraint in the projection of its power [italics in original].[2]

Here in a nutshell are the major reasons that Soviet proxy involvement and activities in Central America and the Caribbean are so seldom even mentioned—as well as the reasons why they are so successful in many respects. The premises of the liberal establishment and of much of the U.S. public concerning Central America and the Caribbean can be summarized as follows:

☐ The U.S. can and should avoid treating the region as an area of confrontation with the USSR, and it can do so by unilateral action.

☐ Change is inevitable and it inevitably involves a diminishing of U.S. influence and advantages for the USSR and Cuba. The latter two aspects need not be a security threat to the United States, albeit that the factors of such change are implicitly recognized as Marxist (why, otherwise, would they be hostile to the United States *and* to the advantage of the USSR and Cuba?).[3] (The distance is short indeed from this view of change to the Marxist claim of representing progress and the inevitable course of history.)

☐ Revolutionary change in the short term is the only road to long-term stability, which is alleged to be the aim of undefined Latin Americans and the ideal goal of the United States. The logical convolution manifest here (that is, change now will be stability tomorrow) can only be explained by the apparent belief that change occurs inevitably in Central America because of the nature of the status quo (presumably "injustice, poverty, repression"). Ironically, if revolutionary change under the banner of the Leninist credo does occur in the region, history argues that it will indeed result in immutable stability—of the type existing today in the USSR, Cuba, and Eastern Europe. That the Latin Americans would like to seek such stability is far less certain if one refers to the majority of people in the area.

☐ In order to encourage change and ensure future stability, the United States should refrain from using force in Central America and the Caribbean. The implication, spelled out in the overwhelming majority of political statements, academic studies, and articles published in the last few years, is that the crisis in Central America today is not military in nature and therefore cannot and should not be met with military power or involvement by the United States. Conversely, because the crisis is not military in nature, it does not by itself represent a security threat to the United States—unless the latter transforms it into a military conflict by misguidedly projecting power into the region. The clearest exposition of such beliefs was provided by Congressmen Gerry E. Studds, Barbara Ann Mikulski, and Robert Edgar, who, in referring to El Salvador, said "The opposition in El Salvador is currently a very diverse group, but we in the United States have the capacity to unite them, to bring together Marxists and non-Marxists; guerrillas and those who abhor the use of violence; the religious and the non-believers; the educated and the poor; the Christian Democrats and the socialists. Yes, we have the power to unite them in opposition to ourselves, or to any policy which provides arms to those who use such weapons to make economic and social progress in El Salvador impossible."[4]

The prevailing opinion on the nature of and solutions to the crisis in Central America can be abridged as follows: The crisis in Central America is revolutionary, spreading, and, sometimes but not always or permanently leftist; but it is grounded in native conditions and represents the wave of the future. The aims of the revolutionaries are nationalistic and center on economic and social progress. Unless the United States forces them into the arms of Cuba and the USSR by militarily intervening in the region—directly or by aiding local governments threatened by the revolutionary wind of change—they will not pose a threat to U.S. security or basic national interests.

It is only in light of these perceptions in the United States, and particularly in the U.S. media and Congress, that the *methods* of proxy employed by the USSR can be understood. Only a clear understanding of the roots and nature of the Central American and Caribbean revolutionary groups will permit an accurate assessment of the scope of the proxy network at Soviet disposal. And a realization that such proxy activities are based on a *network* of groups, individuals, interests, and governments is necessary to understand the effectiveness of (and difficulty of countering the) Soviet proxy involvement. Each of these elements reinforces the others, and none can be understood without clarifying its links to the other two.

The Roots and Nature of the Revolutionary Groups

If there is a place in the world that consistently disproves the myth of the declining role and attraction of ideology, and of Marxism-Leninism in particular, it is Latin America and, to only a slightly lesser extent, the English-speaking Caribbean. In defining the role of Marxism in Latin America, Venezuelan writer Carlos Rangel correctly wrote that Marxism "offers a cosmic vision, and can therefore act as a unifying force. Moreover, its pole of attraction lies . . . in a power that is the very tangible, present-day rival of the United States: the Soviet Union . . . It has been amply proven that the failures of Marxism in no way lessen its seductive power."[5] This would not be new were it not tied to the well-established fact that Latin America is also "the last region of the globe where educated people who have access to all necessary information continue (or claim to do so) to believe that everything unpleasant in Latin America is the result of external agents (North American imperialism or—the reverse of the same medal—the international communist conspiracy)."[6]

Although anti-Americanism has been a general cultural trait of Latin American elites during the past century, Marxism-Leninism today serves as its reinforcement and means of effective articulation. The extraordinary scope of Marxism's attractiveness in Latin America explains the even wider scope of the communist proxy network on the continent.

Almost all Latin American universities, at least since the mid-1960s, have been centers of radicalism; in the overwhelming majority of cases, radicalism takes the shape of various Marxist tendencies, from Trotskyism to Maoism and from vintage-1960s Castroism to orthodox Soviet-style Leninism. Generations of young Latin Americans have been educated in such an environment, and many more have become acquainted with Marxism while studying abroad—in the United States, Western Europe, and, of course, the communist countries. It is thus no coincidence that although all guerrilla leaders in Latin America are Marxists, most are also former university students (generally dropouts) or teachers.

The Catholic church itself, in many cases and countries, is heavily influenced by Marxism—either overtly, with priests engaging in guerrilla warfare or working on behalf of Marxist guerrillas, or, more often, under the generic label of liberation theology. The first case is both self-explanatory and increasingly frequent. Camilo Torres, the Colombian priest and scion of a wealthy family, became the first "martyr" of the revolutionary church while a leader of Castroite guerrillas in his country. Since then, the number of Catholic and Protestant clergy joining the Marxist insurgents has steadily grown. A Belgian-born priest, Rogelio Ponceel, is a prominent ideologue of the virulently Leninist People's Revolutionary Army (ERP) in El Salvador; Canadian priest James Carney was killed in Honduras in 1983 while second in command of the (formerly Trotskyist) Revolutionary Party of Central American Workers (PRTC); and, in Guatemala, Jesuit Carlos Pellecer Faena was a prominent leader of the Guerrilla Army of the Poor (EGP) and the Irish Jesuit McKenna was active in the Guatemalan Organization of the People in Arms (ORPA). Far more important is the role of those in the Catholic clergy who do not openly join the guerrillas but, instead, legitimize them in the eyes of the population by supporting or echoing their propaganda. Most explicit was the statement of the Mexican Bishop of Cuernavaca, Sergio Mendez Arceo: "Only socialism can enable Latin America to achieve true development . . . I believe that a socialist system is more in accord with the Christian principles of true brotherhood, justice, and peace . . . I do not know what kind of socialism, but this is the direction Latin America should go. For myself, I believe it should be a democratic socialism."[7]

Thus, although the Cuernavaca bishop personally may prefer democratic socialism, he considers *any kind of socialism* the desired and likely system in

Latin America. It is natural, if ironic, that the USSR feels compelled to defend the Catholic clergy in Latin America against the United States: "The Reagan Administration has unleashed a noisy, and let us say straight out, unseemly campaign against the Catholic Church of the countries of Central America. Many representatives of the church in this region support the national liberation struggle of the peoples against pro-Washington bloody dictatorships. This has aroused the fit of anger on the part of the Washington Administrators."[8]

The revolutionary church is today openly promoted by the Sandinista regime in Nicaragua as the *true* "Popular Church," as opposed to the Catholic hierarchy. This church, together with the thoroughly radicalized university faculties and student bodies (Rangel's books were burnt on the campus of the University of Caracas), and many of the socialist, social democratic, and Christian Democratic leaders in Latin America share at least one essential ideological trait—their universal acceptance of and belief in the dependency theories, some of whose main representatives (Andre Gunder Frank and Celso Furtado) are Latin American. Although basically a neo-Marxist development of Lenin's own simplistic analysis of imperialism, the *dependencia* theories also answer the Latin American cultural envy and frustration expressed by anti-Americanism. Such theories strengthen the messianic appeal of the revolutionaries, who promise a free and prosperous Latin America—once dependence on American imperialism is broken. The *dependencia* theories channel discontent with the accomplishments of existing revolutionary regimes away from the leadership. The statement of the Nicaraguan regime in April 1981, in response to the U.S. decision to cancel present and future cheap loans and food aid, is a case in point: "The economic cooperation that the United States has agreed to offer to our people . . . was never regarded as a bonus or a gift. We must recall that our country was impoverished by the indiscriminate looting by foreign companies and by the voraciousness of a family which protected and built its power on the support it always received from the United States. Therefore, the loans received were only a very small part of a pending debt. The Nicaraguan government is preparing to denounce at international forums this unjustified aggression."[9] Claims that poverty, injustice, and the absence of democracy in Central America are all due to the United States are even more virulent when they come from the Marxist groups still out of power. This in turn raises the issue of the aims of those groups—as well as those of the revolutionary regimes, whether in Grenada, Nicaragua, or anywhere else.

The common denominator of all Marxist-Leninist groups in Central America since their inception, and regardless of their feuds, has been their open, consistent, and deeply felt belief that the United States is their main enemy. As *the* enemy, the United States has played an essential role in unifying such competing elements as Trotskyites, Maoists, Castroites, and orthodox Marxists. The realization that the external support necessary to conquer power would come only from the USSR and its satellites was the necessary corollary of a rapidly spreading conviction among the revolutionaries in Central America that victory required a regional and ultimately global perspective that put aside doctrinal differences. These factors were clearly demonstrated in the cases of both Nicaragua and El Salvador.

The statements and actions of the Sandinist National Liberation Front (FSLN) in Nicaragua since it seized state power in July 1979 provide a perfect example of the natural linkage between anti-Americanism and pro-Soviet positions in a Marxist-Leninist political environment. Not only did the FSLN immediately introduce a new national anthem defining the *yanquis* as "enemies of mankind," but it also started building the largest military force in the history of Central America, under the pretext of a possible future conflict with the United States. At the same time, as a corollary of such attitudes and perceptions, Nicaragua openly supported the Soviet invasion of Afghanistan at the end of 1979, and a few months later the FSLN and the Soviet Communist Party signed a formal agreement on party-to-party relations.

The Salvadoran guerrillas are even more outspoken in their fundamental and irreconcilable opposition to the United States and all the values it represents. Thus, the ERP supreme leader, who is today the main military chief of the Salvadoran guerrilla umbrella, the Farabundo Marti National Liberation Front (FMLN), clearly stated that:

> To talk about our position in the international field means talking about the struggle against the North American imperialism, which we consider the fundamental enemy of all revolutionary peoples and movements . . . we value the great contributions which in this period have brought the Indochinese peoples, specifically the Vietnamese people, which has obtained the greatest victory, pushing back the imperialist policy [and] placing imperialism in a situation of weakness . . . the identity of having a common enemy, defeated and weakened by the people of Vietnam, has made possible the victory of the Nicaraguan people and will make possible the triumph of the Salvadoran Revolution and that of Central America . . . We consider ourselves together with the revolutionary forces of Latin America in general, and of Central America in particular, and with a very special place to the Cuban Revolution, as fundamental and strategic allies of the Salvadoran Revolution . . . [10]

The leadership of the Farabundo Marti People's Liberation Forces (FPL— the oldest, once the largest, and now the second-largest guerrilla group in El Salvador) was equally clear in this respect: "The United States has never asked authorization to invade Latin America. It is time that our peoples tighten ranks against the *main enemy*. The revolution in Central America is one, is indivisible, and the Salvadoran [revolutionary] process cannot and should not deal in an isolated manner from, or on the fringes of, those [processes] taking place in

Guatemala and Honduras" (italics added).[11] FPL leader "Isabel" went further, stating that "this struggle advancing in the Isthmus, first and foremost as a result of the triumph of the Nicaraguan people, has transformed Central America into true revolutionary *foco*. It is because of this that our organization has as a fundamental point in its strategy the Central Americanization of the struggle."[12]

Not only is the United States the main enemy and the cause of all problems facing Central and Latin America—but the United States does so as a result of and in order to alleviate its own internal "contradictions." As the Guatemalan extreme leftist group, the People's Revolutionary Movement (MRP-IXIM), expressed it, "*The U.S. imperialists, in bloody unity with the very rich and their genocidal armies, caused the economic, political and social crisis that our peoples are experiencing* . . . These gringo enemies have promoted wars, for the purpose of alleviating their profound internal crisis, by arming and training puppet armies to massacre the peoples who are struggling for their national and social liberation" (italics in original).[13] It was the same Joaquin Villalobos who articulately brought together anti-Americanism, Leninism, dependency theory, and the leftist interpretation of recent global trends and developments. Asked what the international policy of the ERP is, Villalobos replied:

> . . . By defining ourselves as enemies of the North American imperialism, we identify ourselves also with the cause of the nonaligned movement, with the struggle of the Palestinian people, and of the liberation movements of the African peoples . . . In general we identify ourselves with the cause of all oppressed and exploited peoples.[14]

Villalobos's list of motivations, models, and examples for the ERP includes many shared by other revolutionary groups throughout Central America. Factionalism in the guerrilla groups in Central America has long been interpreted as a serious obstacle to Soviet influence over them. Since the late 1970s, however, factions have become less significant and, to the extent that such differences persist, are additional assets in the Soviet proxy network.

Revolutionary violence has been the most important issue facing the Central American Marxists since the 1960s and the source of most debates, conflicts and clashes within the left. The Communist parties (CPs), for decades the only organized force of the Marxist left in Central America, were totally submissive, if minor, tools of the Soviet Union. Their cadres were trained in the USSR and the Soviet bloc, their leaders were selected on Moscow's orders, and their tactics and positions were decided, sometimes in minute detail, by the Kremlin.

Central American CPs penetrated elements of the military and attempted to ride to power following coups. Under such circumstances, Fabio Castillo

Figueroa, then probably a member of the Salvadoran Communist Party (PCES) and a vocal supporter of the Cuban Revolution, became a member of the short-lived junta that ruled El Salvador between October 1960 and January 25, 1961. Previously, the Guatemalan Labor (Communist) Party (PGT) had also been successful in penetrating, infiltrating, and ultimately controlling the Arbenz regime in Guatemala between 1950 and 1954—again, by riding on the back of a particular military faction led by Arbenz himself. The Cuban Revolution did little to change this favorite approach of the Communist parties; on the contrary, most CPs regarded Castro as an aberration and a dangerous "left-wing adventurist," a label even more strongly applied to Ernesto "Che" Guevara.

"Left-wing adventurist" or not, Castro had one powerful argument that lured large numbers of sympathizers and would-be imitators throughout Latin America: his success in taking power. For the purposes of the present study, Castro's impact on Central America and the Caribbean may be defined as follows:

☐ Castroites advocated revolutionary violence and pro-Moscow leaders either rejected it or saw it as secondary or tactical in nature, thus causing repeated splits in the ranks of orthodox Communist parties. The difference of opinion was summarized in 1967 by the Guatemalan FAR (Rebel Armed Forces), which broke with the PGT, claiming that "the PGT supplied the ideas and FAR supplied the dead." Such splits, occurring until the mid-1970s in El Salvador and Honduras and as recently as 1980 in Guatemala, weakened Soviet influence in the region and further reduced the already small ranks of the CPs. Such splits were magnified in their impact on the size and influence of the CPs. They eroded the USSR's ability to influence the left in the face of the additional splits resulting from Sino-Soviet disputes.

☐ After the 1968 domestication of Castro by the Soviets—demonstrated by Castro's support for the invasion of Czechoslovakia; the collapse of Castroite guerrillas in Venezuela, Peru, and Guatemala; and by Guevara's Bolivian fiasco—the Castroites were without any significant external source of support. The pro-Chinese groups (the only significant one, the Peruvian Shining Path, is Maoist but hostile to the present Chinese leadership) continued to decline, as did the Trotskyites. The ideological, tactical, and strategic impact of these developments was decisive throughout Latin America.

Ideologically, it became clear that neither the orthodox CPs nor the Castroites had a credible blueprint for achieving power in Latin America. The "legal" and "peaceful" means preferred by the CPs had been discredited by the fall of Allende in 1973. Tactically, it became equally clear that neither urban-oriented violence (in Uruguay, Brazil, Argentina, or Chile) nor a strictly rural approach (in Guatemala, Nicaragua before the mid-1970s, or Colombia) could succeed alone. Strategically, it dawned on Moscow and its Latin American proxies that the post-Vietnam global position of the United States presented significant opportunities in Latin America. Those opportunities, however, could not be exploited unless ideological premises, tactics, and approaches were radically altered. New methods were first used and proven successful in the Nicaraguan civil war in 1978–1979; they have been further refined since and are near perfection in El Salvador. The success of these methods was made possible by the combination of post-Vietnam changes in the U.S.-USSR global balance of power, the spectacular revival of Cuba's ability to attract Soviet support on behalf of her own updated Latin American strategy (made possible by Castro's role in Angola and the Horn of Africa), and the triumph of the Sandinistas. Although the Soviets themselves seldom are explicit about the scope and method of their role in Latin America and the Caribbean, at least some Central American guerrilla groups are not so reticent. It is revealing, therefore, to examine the guerrillas' own perceptions of their activities and their role in the global geopolitical conflict between East and West, in the region and in Latin America as a whole. The basic text for such an analysis is the *International Declaration* of the Guatemalan EGP. The EGP is by far the largest Guatemalan guerrilla force, the most sophisticated in tactics and propaganda operations; its very history makes it an avatar of Central American revolutionary groups.[15]

Perceptions and Scope of Proxy Activities

The EGP defines its strategy as "people's revolutionary war [that] is part and consequence of the world struggle between the capitalist system on one side, and the forces of socialism and national liberation on the other."[16] The heavy influence of the Vietnamese war, defined by Giap and Ho Chi Minh as a "people's revolutionary war," can be read here, together with the perception of Guatemala as part of a global conflict. With the guerrillas seeing themselves as part of a global communist tide, it is indeed difficult to see how the United States could separate the Central American conflict from the East-West one.

In the EGP's view, the global developments strengthening its chances of victory are the following:

> Parallel to this crisis within the capitalist system, a process of readjustment and revitalization of their revolutionary positions has been taking place among the powers in the world socialist camp. The Soviet Union, among other socialist countries, appears to have ended a period of impasse which created much confusion, and to have returned its foreign policy to the

militant, combative stance which it should have by nature. In spite of painful developments within the socialist camp, such as the traitorous abandonment of revolutionary principles by the Chinese Communist Party, and the contradictions springing up among the European communist parties, the global camp of revolution and socialism has taken heart and encouragement from the popular and revolutionary victories in Asia, Africa and Latin America.[17]

The importance of such a statement is both far-reaching and impossible to overestimate. It implies or spells out the following essential developments:

☐ The USSR, at a time when the Carter administration was struggling to maintain détente and to have SALT II approved (that is, months before the invasion of Afghanistan), had departed from its previous ambiguous stance in Latin America convincingly enough to receive the approval of the EGP. The EGP had publicly dismissed the pro-Soviet PGT as irrelevant if not treacherous and viewed the Soviets themselves as vacillating and responsible for confusion in the revolutionary ranks. Any Chinese role in Latin America was over by 1979, due to the de-Maoization process led by Deng Xiaoping.

☐ Eurocommunism did result at least temporarily in a weakening of support from the European Communist parties for the Central American guerrillas—an indication that such support did exist previously.

☐ Vietnam, Angola, and Nicaragua (the "victories" in Asia, Africa, and Latin America) have dramatically raised the expectations of the Central American guerrillas. They presented a global image of "accelerated change in the correlation of forces, in favor of the forces of socialism and national liberation."[18]

An additional and equally fundamental change in the Americas was the new Cuban role, described by the EGP as follows:

Revolutionary Cuba has sent reverberations throughout the hemisphere by taking the role of the socialist vanguard in this part of the world . . . The Cuban Revolution is becoming more important today. Its existence favors alliances between democratic countries that want to resist the rapacity and expansionist maneuvers of imperialism in Latin America.[19]

In other words, Cuba is reasserting its role, temporarily lost at the end of the 1960s. This time, however, Cuba is not an isolated revolutionary example for the guerrillas but is the vanguard, that is, the spearhead of global communism in the western hemisphere. Such a role clearly implies that Cuba represents and receives the help of global Soviet resources. Clear demonstration of Castroism's new life is provided by the outlawed (by the Guatemalan left) MRP-IXIM: "The Cuban revolution marked the beginning of revolutionary processes in Latin America, showing the *true and definitive path* by which to expel the gringo imperialists" (italics added).[20]

The EGP claim that Cuba facilitates alliances between democratic countries sharing an anti-U.S. view clearly refers to countries such as Mexico, Ecuador, Grenada (before 1983), and obviously Nicaragua; all joined Cuba in supporting revolutionary causes in Central America (for the 1978–1979 period, Panama and Costa Rica also cooperated closely with Cuba in support of the Sandinista insurgents). The fact that Cuba retains its magnetic attraction for such mutually hostile groups as the EGP and MRP-IXIM is itself an indication of Havana's unique role in the Americas.

Examining the Central American situation, the EGP clearly saw the region as "the weakest link in the continental imperialist chain," a Leninist concept alternatively applied to one country or another in the region.[21] Rafael Menjívar, a noted Salvadoran Marxist and a member of the ERP as well as of the political front FDR (Democratic Revolutionary Front), wrote a tract entitled *El Salvador: El Eslabón Mas Pequeño* (El Salvador: The Smallest Link). In Leninist logic, the weakest link, or the smallest, is the best target for communist takeover—hence the concentration of global Soviet proxy resources in Central America. This concentration was made even more necessary and immediate by the impact of the Nicaraguan events. As the same EGP stated, "The victorious Sandinista revolution has produced a qualitative change in the area, a spirit impossible to negate and much too powerful to have been checked at Nicaragua's borders. It has brought about immense changes, among which the following can be singled out because of their significance: (1) A clear shift in the correlation of forces in favor of revolution and popular aspirations. (2) Revolutionary armed struggle as a way to power has become the order of the day and has acquired unquestionable validity in the entire area."[22]

To conclude, the guerrillas in Central America perceive that the time has come for the establishment of a chain of Marxist regimes on the isthmus. This perception is based on global developments as well as continental realities, the most important of which is Soviet reassessment of support for revolutionary violence. The guerrillas view revolutionary activities in Guatemala, Honduras, and El Salvador as inseparable from the consolidation of the Sandinista regime. And the Sandinistas cannot consolidate their control over Nicaragua unless guerrillas in other countries increase in strength. The spearhead of global communist pressures in Central and Latin America and the Caribbean is a reactivated Cuba. It is thus important to examine to what extent statements like the EGP's translate into practice at two levels—within the communist universe, and between Communists (that is, Marxist-Leninists) and non-Marxists; that is, what are the *methods* of Marxist-Leninist activities in Central America and the Caribbean?

Methods

The most effective change in the Marxist approach in Central America is the trend toward homogenization and coordination, at the national and regional levels. Continental and global groups and umbrella organizations, radical governments, Western groups, and Soviet bloc states have all been drawn into the network.

Homogenization occurs at the national level among groups with historically different interpretations of Marxism (Castroites, Maoists, Trotskyites, pro-Soviet orthodox Communists), and regionally it is manifest in the repetition of patterns of behavior and the closest possible ties between groups of different national origins. Homogenization as a dominant trend is particularly relevant to Soviet proxy activities, since it increases confusion among outside observers. Note the often-heard Western claim that the differences between the guerrillas and their allies (among socialists, social-democrats, or Christian Democrats) and differences within or between the guerrilla groups eliminate any possibility of manipulation from abroad or coordination of actions.

National-level homogenization is manifest in all Central American countries and takes the form of a rapid and steady decline in the level of ideological conflict between Trotskyites, Maoists, Castroites, and orthodox Communists. Most significant in this respect were the "unifications" of the three factions of the FSLN on March 3, 1979, and the establishment of the FMLN in El Salvador in 1980. In the first case, the practitioners of the "protracted popular war" (GPP, *guerra popular prolongada*), the insurrectionists and urban terrorists of the *tercerista* faction, and the ultra-Leninists of the "proletarian" tendency, who were expelled from the FSLN in 1975 by the founder of the movement, Carlos Fonseca Amador, all found their way to unity on an equal basis by closely coordinating tactics and strategy and peacefully sharing power after the July 1979 victory. The fact that the unification was very much a shotgun marriage imposed by Havana and encouraged by the universal expectation of victory over Somoza should not mislead—the date of the unification, coming barely four months before Somoza's fall and after four years of public differences, indicates that all was not smooth. Nonetheless, the fact that unification did occur and that the coalition has since grown more stable demonstrates the effectiveness of Cuban pressure.

In the second case, the FMLN's formation was even more of a spectacular feat, if one believes, on the basis of most available evidence, that the Marxist left in El Salvador is historically fragmented along deep separation lines. The

FMLN unification brought together in a steadily advancing process the following groups: the PCES, the ancestor of all other violent groups in the country and a party that was part of the government as late as the first junta following the October 1979 coup; the ERP, which was involved in killing PCES cadres during the 1970s and greeted the October junta with a failed but bloody attempt at insurrection; the FARN (Armed Forces of National Resistance), born in 1975 as a result of the ERP's murder of its initial ideologue, Roque Dalton, and the attempted murder of its founder, Ernesto Jovel (Jovel did die in suspicious circumstances in 1980, at a time of renewed FARN-ERP tensions); the PRTC (the Salvadoran branch), which started in 1976 as a Trotskyite group with regional pretensions and included former PCES cadres, including Fabio Castillo, and present leader Roberto Roca, as well as dissatisfied FARN cadres; and, finally, the FPL, at the time still led by its founder, former PCES secretary general Salvador Cayetano Carpio, who left the party over the issue of guerrilla warfare and personally disliked the present PCES leader, Shafik Jorge Handal (who replaced Carpio in the top party job). Carpio distrusted the ERP and PCES equally—the first for the ambitions of its leader, Villalobos, and its unstructured organization; the second for its status as a Soviet puppet and a bourgeois group of opportunists. Four of these five groups thus had in common a strong dislike and mistrust of the PCES. The PCES reacted to the 1979 October coup by trying either to join it or to push the military further left (an effort joined by the FARN). Meanwhile the ERP tried to take advantage of the confusion following the coup to seize power. The FPL treated the whole affair as irrelevant in light of the reformist nature of the rebel military. Nevertheless, less than a month after the collapse of the first junta (January 1980), the FPL, PCES, and FARN joined in the Revolutionary Coordination of the Masses (CRM). They were later joined by the ERP and PRTC.

Similar developments took place in Honduras in April 1983. Six groups on the Marxist-Leninist left, once again including the Communist party (PCH) that initially spawned them all, formed the National Unified Leadership of the Honduran Revolutionary Movement (DNU-MRH). These were preceded by the Guatemalan guerrilla groups FAR, EGP, and ORPA, which, together with a minority faction of the PGT, formed the National Revolutionary Unity of Guatemala (URNG) in January 1982. Unification in the case of Guatemala again welded groups with competing histories and a long tradition of mutual distrust: the FAR, with its old clashes with the PGT and Castroite tradition of the 1960s; the EGP, initially a FAR splinter, with a quasi-Maoist, allegedly Indian-oriented protracted warfare strategy; ORPA, another FAR spinoff mostly comprised of intellectuals trying to use the Indians as Marxist revolutionary cannon fodder; and the National Leadership Nucleus, minority members of the PGT central committee and Politburo, who joined the guerrilla tactics despite the opposition of the majority *camarilla* faction.

All these developments (except those in Nicaragua) share their inclusion of the Communist parties, in toto or at least a faction—the most obvious indication of Moscow's strategic change of attitude in Central America. These events dramatically prove the disappearance of all relevant ideological distinctions between the various shades of the violent left. When Trotskyites, Maoists, Castroites, and orthodox Communists join—and actually coordinate operations and tactics and, at least in El Salvador, submit to the field command of leaders from other groups—the only conclusion to be drawn is that ideological nuances are irrelevant or at least submerged into the great tide of the Marxist-Leninist revolutionary offensive.

Although these are general traits of the homogenization process at a national level, similar trends dominate the guerrilla-oriented left at the regional level. This process developed from the manifestations of "internationalism" that brought EGP, ORPA, and FAR elements into Nicaragua to fight against Somoza in 1978–1979; caused FAR cadres to participate in the first FPL kidnappings in El Salvador in the early 1970s; and brought ERP, FARN, and FPL members into the ranks of the FMLN in El Salvador and of the EGP and ORPA in Guatemala.

Since then, the cooperation among varying Marxist groups within national boundaries has reached a level that enables them to cooperate with groups in neighboring countries. As seen above, the Central American, continental, and global character of Marxist operations in Central American states was always underscored by prominent leftist leaders in Guatemala, El Salvador, and Nicaragua. As a result, regional strategic cooperation has been a fact since at least 1979, when the Sandinistas were helped to victory by a wide spectrum of leftist elements throughout the region. What is relatively new, and obvious since 1981–1982, is the immediate tactical field coordination in military operations and the consistent propaganda coordination among guerrillas in El Salvador, Guatemala, Honduras, the regime in Nicaragua, and their fellow travelers and sympathizers in the West—as well as in Cuba, the Warsaw Pact nations, and Soviet satellites throughout the world.

Regionally, the best example of the coordination among the Marxist guerrillas was provided by Octavio Perez, a main leader of the Honduran Morazanist Front for the Liberation of Honduras (FMLH): "If it becomes necessary to fight against the Honduran Army in order to defend the Nicaraguan revolution, then one must fight; and if it becomes necessary to fight in order to keep Honduran military units from going into El Salvador, then we are willing to do that also."[23] Similar open admissions of tactical military cooperation were provided by both ORPA and the EGP. These groups claim to have initiated major operations against the Guatemalan government during major FMLN offensives in order to prevent Guatemala from aiding El Salvador; they actually did so at times that were clearly inopportune for themselves, thus resulting in major losses.

Furthermore, both the Nicaraguan regime and the FMLN have succeeded in actually creating Honduran revolutionary groups—the FMLH and the MPL-Cinchoneros (Popular Liberation Movement). Actually, the Cinchoneros were more of an ERP creation.

A spectacular example of close coordination across national boundaries took place in August 1982. After a number of top ERP leaders were captured in Tegucigalpa, the Cinchoneros, in their most dramatic action to date, kidnapped most of the members of the San Pedro Sula chamber of commerce. The guerrillas then conditioned the release of their captives on the ERP commanders' secure passage out of Honduras. In a chain reaction, the MRP-IXIM kidnapped the daughter of Honduran president Suazo Cordoba in December 1982 in Guatemala—as a protest against Honduran hostility toward the Nicaraguan regime, FMLN operations on Honduran territory, and Honduras's unwillingness to allow Guatemalan guerrillas on its territory. In September 1984, just prior to the expected FMLN offensive timed for the U.S. elections, the URNG had already started its own major operations, clearly aimed at tying the hands of the Guatemalan government, in case the Salvadoran fighting threatened the latter or even spilled over into Guatemala. Finally, and most important, amid a major offensive against the Managua regime by the anti-Sandinista guerrillas, Nicaragua unleashed what proved to be the first wave of Honduran guerrillas—a 97-man PRTC unit invaded Honduras from Nicaragua and, after a brief existence in the jungles of the Olancho Department, was wiped out by the Honduran military. The action was clearly intended both as a warning to Honduras for allowing the *contras* to use its territory and as a maneuver to occupy the Honduran army at a time of extensive FMLN operations at the Honduras–El Salvador border. Once again, in September 1984, a new wave of Nicaraguan-trained and -armed insurgents apparently penetrated Honduras in connection with an expected FMLN offensive.

The homogenization of the Marxist guerrillas and the coordination of field operations that it has facilitated are also evident in the realm of civilian leftist or reformist groups in the region. The tactics are not only similar—they are often an exact copy of tactics pursued by other groups or guerrillas in a neighboring country.

By far the most effective and most frequently used tactic is that of the united front. Both the "united front from above" and the "united front from below" are consistently pursued on the national and international levels. To a decisive extent, all these fronts operate as little more than political or propaganda proxies for the guerrillas of El Salvador and Guatemala, for the Nicaraguan regime, and ultimately for the socialist camp led by the USSR.

The "united front from above" approach is characterized by political alliances at the leadership level between Marxist guerrilla groups and non-Marxist or non-Leninist (nontotalitarian) groups. Historically, the most accomplished practitioner of this approach has been the PCES, as demonstrated by its highly effective electoral alliances with the Christian Democrats and the minuscule Social Democrats (MNR) during the 1970s, under the umbrella of the National Opposition Union (UNO). The FSLN *tercerista* faction also practiced such an approach successfully, under the label of Large Opposition Front (FAO). In both cases, non- or even anti-Marxist groups closely cooperated with the Marxist-Leninists in the name of democratic action against dictatorship, but they retained their institutional and ideological identities. Moreover, in both cases the fronts collapsed when the question of immediate sharing of power became acute—the Christian Democrats in El Salvador became the government in opposition to the Marxist-Leninists and guerrilla organizatons, and the democratic parties of FAO became the anti-FSLN opposition (political, military, or both). As long as such fronts existed, however, the main (sometimes the only) beneficiaries were the Marxist-Leninists. They received public exposure and increased legitimacy through elections or legal political roles. Able to operate freely, they expanded their meager membership—in the case of the PCES by some 80 percent during the 1970s—and posed as legitimate political forces, acceptable to and compatible with a democratic system. In Central America the clergy, particularly the Catholic clergy committed to liberation theology, played a role comparable to that of political lay organizations by establishing what practially amounted to united fronts with the Leninist left.

Internationally, "united front from above" tactics were pursued successfully by the FSLN and the FMLN (the latter through its FDR front) in wooing such non-Marxist but leftist forces as the Socialist International (S.I.). The MNR, a minor member of the FDR (it has one out of seven votes in the FDR leadership, despite Guillermo Ungo's position as nominal head of the FDR), is an S.I. member; the FSLN is consistently admitted in S.I. meetings as a de facto part-time member. Although the S.I. is far from united in support of the revolutionary left in Central America, most of its spokesmen, together with important member parties like the German and Swedish social democrats, are in support.

The importance of international propaganda activities for the Central American left is underscored by the high priority it receives and by its enormous scope. An ORPA leader stated that "ORPA also has an *international front* which, in addition to publicizing its work maintains close ties with international revolutionary organizations" (italics added).[24] The very term "front" indicates both the quasi-military and strategic importance given to propaganda (ORPA's operational areas are also named fronts), and its deceptive, disinformational content. As for the scope of such propaganda, Villalobos claimed correctly that "we have organized a large solidarity apparatus that encompasses the entire planet, even in the United States, where one of the most active centers of solidarity exists."[25] Maurice Bishop of Grenada, during one of his many speeches warning of an imminent U.S. attack, also claimed that in such an event the "fight can take place on two *fronts*, the first being in the military field and the second meaning that 'We can also fight back successfully if, instead of having to face Grenada, a small country . . . the imperialists are made to face a force of 3 billion strong as we build a powerful, worldwide anti-imperialist alliance'" (italics added).[26]

At the level of the "united front from below," the Central American Marxists operate along well-known Leninist patterns—steadily infiltrating low- and middle-level ranks of other institutions, parties, or organizations, and thus subverting the authority of their freely chosen top leaders. Minuscule groups are also included in guerrilla-dominated fronts for their propaganda value—the best example is the small splinter of the Christian Democratic Party of El Salvador, led by Ruben Zamora, and the MNR of Guillermo Ungo. Both are FDR members, and both lack any political or military strength in El Salvador but are active internationally for the FDR as "democrats" legitimizing the Leninists in the eyes of the West. Isolated personalities play a similar role. The most prominent cases are the revolutionary priests, now Sandinista ministers, who allow the FSLN to proclaim its respect for religion and the church. At this point it is only possible to provide an image of the scope and modus operandi of the Soviet proxy assets in Central America and the Caribbean, based on the major characteristics of the situation in the region; the nature, tactics, and perceptions of the revolutionary groups; and the interconnection of all these elements.

THE SOVIET PROXY NETWORK

Structure and Membership

The members of the proxy network in Central America and the Caribbean fluctuate in membership, differ over specific issues, and vary in their interconnections. Some members are temporary, some permanent; some are united by their strategic aims, some by immediate considerations or a vague community of perceived interests. Membership itself, and the role various members play at specific times, can be defined according to (1) ideology, (2) institutional nature, (3) location, (4) specific role, and (5) degree of autonomy from Soviet control.

Ideology. The members of the network may be roughly divided into Marxist-Leninists, radicals of various shades, socialists, social democrats, or just loosely defined "progressives"; the main distinction between the first type and all the others is in the Marxists' strategic aims and degree of attachment to the USSR and its manifest regional proxies. Thus, the Marxist-Leninists' specific and public aims are (1) the destruction of the free-market system and the democratic political process, or at least the chance of democracy in the region and (2) the elimination of all U.S. influence in any form. All these aims are identical to or at least closely connected to the USSR's global strategic goals. The radical, leftist, or simply anti-American members of the network are united in their mutual opposition to the governments targeted by the Marxist-Leninists and in their hostility to U.S. influence in the region. These members do not generally cooperate with the USSR, consciously act on Soviet advice, or try to promote Soviet aims.

Institutional nature.   Network members may be nongovernmental institutions, national or international in character; subnational groups operating against or outside government policies; or governments.

Location.   The network members may be national, regional, continental, or global (that is, outside the western hemisphere).

Specific role.   The role played by a particular network member may be a strictly legitimizing one, that is, centered on propaganda, political and diplomatic, as well as moral support; or it may be financial and military support or direct involvement in Marxist-Leninist violent activities (whether in the region or outside it on behalf of regional actors).

Degree of autonomy from Soviet control.   Network members may be simple extensions of Soviet operations, semiautonomous actors, autonomous actors, or independent or coincidental actors. Moreover, the network's complex structure requires further distinctions regarding the level of known or public links to the USSR. Thus, a country like Cuba is clearly a Soviet proxy with a high, but still limited, degree of autonomy in regional affairs; Nicaragua is far more directly a Cuban proxy than a Soviet one; the FMLN is a combined Cuban-Nicaraguan and Soviet proxy; certain guerrilla groups, like the Cinchoneros or the FMLH in Honduras, are primarily FMLN or Nicaraguan proxies. Certain organizations, such as the mushrooming "committees of solidarity with the people of El Salvador" (CISPES) in the United States and Western Europe are basically proxies of the FDR, in itself a front for the FMLN. One may thus define the Cinchoneros of Honduras as proxies of the FMLN— which is often a proxy of Nicaragua, itself largely a Cuban proxy, with Cuba a Soviet proxy. Naturally, a group like the Cinchoneros, five times removed from the Kremlin, presents the Soviet Union with both opportunities—mostly deniability and deception—and problems of control. Control is particularly difficult because each intermediate proxy has a degree of autonomy and specific tactical, if not strategic, goals that may vary from those of the Soviet Politburo.

The Soviet method for magnifying the advantages of proxies and ensuring a significant degree of direct control is the use of umbrella organizations. Thus, although the Cinchoneros were clearly an FMLN creation—for the specific purpose of manipulating the Honduran government and military in order to facilitate FMLN use of that country's territory as a safe rear area and logistical supplies route—the Cinchoneros are also members of the DNU-MRH umbrella, which includes the PCH as a prominent member. The PCH in turn is a direct Soviet proxy; an additional control, the PCES, an FMLN member, is also a direct Soviet proxy, thus enabling the USSR to have a high degree of *direct* intelligence and influence over the Cinchoneros. This is in addition to its overall influence through the Havana-Managua-FMLN proxy chain. The result is that terrorist operations by the Cinchoneros reinforce the effectiveness of the overall network, are deniable because of the obvious FMLN link, but in fact are controllable by Moscow to a significant extent.

The autonomous actors are themselves manipulated in a very definite manner by the Soviets, through the system of proxies mentioned above. The Socialist International is a very good example in this respect, since it is, apparently, an independent actor in Central America. Prominent personalities and member parties of the S.I. are strongly anti-U.S., however. Such attitudes are easily translated into support for such anti-U.S. groups as the FSLN or the Salvadoran FDR. The coincidence of views on the role of the U.S. would have been insufficient to make the S.I. an autonomous, rather than independent, actor, had it not been reinforced by the directly manipulated Soviet proxy chain. Thus, the Grenadan New Jewel Movement before October 1983, the Salvadoran MNR (an FDR member), and the Chilean Socialist Party (PSCh)—all either Marxist-Leninist or known Soviet, Cuban, or combined Soviet-Cuban instruments—are full-fledged S.I. members, share in its decisionmaking, and at the least provide timely intelligence on S.I. activities to Moscow, Havana, and Managua. Documents captured in Grenada clearly indicate that Managua, Havana, St. Georges, and the FDR were all aware of their ability to manipulate the S.I. and prepared to treat it as their own propaganda instrument. Again the double or triple control mechanism employed by the USSR was applied. The Managua joint strategy session regarding the S.I., and involving the NJM, MNR, and the PSCh, was engineered by the FSLN and Havana, with the Soviets directly controlling Havana and heavily influencing the FSLN. Cuba and the FSLN actually control the FMLN, which in turn controls the FDR, of which the MNR is a minor member; in addition, Havana decisively influenced the NJM. Small though the MNR, PSCh, and NJM were, their adoption of a consistent and united strategy within the S.I. and cooperation with the FSLN representatives magnified their role within the organization. Their unity gave coherence and increased effectiveness to their intra-S.I. coalition and alliance policies and indirectly made the USSR a factor in S.I. decisionmaking.

In the realm of autonomous, proxy, or proxy-of-proxy cases, Soviet ability to control the network depends on the members' institutional nature and the actors themselves. Soviet control is characterized by multiple influence mechanisms. Thus, nongovernmental actors such as terrorist groups (the Basque ETA, IRA, PLO, South American groups like the Argentine Montoneros and ERP, the Uruguayan Tupamaros, and the Chilean MIR [Movement of the Revolutionary Left]) are all known to have been trained or financed by, operated on behalf of, or fought together with the FSLN and the FMLN. Again, the USSR cannot and, most importantly, need not control those groups at all points in their trajectory; it is enough to control some of their targeting process, through influence over governments or groups that provide aid, safe areas, or headquarters. Whether the ERP unit under Alfredo Irurzun killed Somoza in Asuncion under orders from Managua, Havana, Moscow, or elsewhere is irrelevant; though proof that the ERP and Irurzun had ties to the FSLN is abundant, the essential factor remains the murder of Anastasio Somoza in perhaps the most tightly controlled anticommunist country in the western hemisphere. The event served to demonstrate the long arm of the FSLN, the omnipresence of the left, and the ability of the network to use anti-Somoza sentiment to legitimize international terrorism.

Although such terrorist groups as the ETA, PLO, IRA, ERP, Montoneros, Tupamaros, and MIR are seen universally as free-lancers, their activities in Central America are a significant addition to the geographic scope, financial strength, and reach of the network. Once again, they allow the USSR a high degree of credible denial while the Soviets publicly boast of supplying fighters, trainers, training facilities, funds, or "solidarity" to the FMLN, URNG, and FSLN. At no significant cost to themselves, the Soviets use and manipulate (even where they do not necessarily control) such groups on behalf of their strategic aims. Once again, Soviet control is exercised through the receiving end of such terrorist activities—the Nicaraguan, Salvadoran, or Cuban proxies.

The network specialization is highly developed, with certain members strictly propaganda-oriented whereas others are politically and militarily centered. This differentiation is directly linked to the front tactics brought to perfection in Central America by the FSLN and particularly by the FMLN. Thus, although military power is concentrated in the hands of self-defined Marxist-Leninists, particular propaganda and deception tasks are performed by non-Marxist figures, groups, or countries. Guillermo Ungo and Ruben Zamora of the FDR—one the social democratic vice-president of the S.I., the other an aspiring member of the Christian Democratic International—are politically irrelevant in El Salvador and badly outnumbered in the FDR decisionmaking process, generally by a factor of three. The FMLN popular organizations (that is, front organizations) number five members out of the seven in the FDR leadership. They receive orders from their respective FMLN guerrilla groups, which tend to be uniform in their decisions. The ERP controls the FPL and part of the FARN; the PCES has tried to take over the PRTC and part of the FARN. The ERP is closest to Havana and Nicaragua; the PCES is a docile Soviet tool.

The interrelationship between various members of the network becomes clear when the Ungos and Zamoras of Central America only represent their respective umbrella organizations in international non-Marxist forums. Their membership in such umbrella organizations as the FDR or URNG subjects them to majority decisionmaking and therefore to the will of the Leninist majority, which is committed to regional strategic aims shared, if not always decided, by the Soviet Union. The Ungos and Zamoras are thus representing or, more precisely, fronting for the Kremlin, whether in the S.I., the United Nations, or the nonaligned movement. Although an Ungo or a Zamora is personally and politically a captive of the network, some actors who are not nevertheless play an analogous role. The most prominent is the "progressive" sector of the Catholic church; that is, the practitioners of liberation theology. They are joined by Western groups defined by proleftist sympathies, anti-Americanism, and religiously based pacifism, such as the American Friends Service Committee, OXFAM, Protestant U.S. elements, and so on. From a Leninist and, incidentally, also from a realistic viewpoint, such groups are objectively members of the network. Much the same applies for at least sectors of such international institutions as the United Nations, the nonaligned movement, or the Human Rights Commissions of the OAS and U.N. In all these cases, the reason or the background for network membership is the same—anti-Marxist governments are open enough to allow their enemies of various shades to collect damning proofs of human-rights violations against those governments while their critics are unable or, more often, unwilling to collect similar proofs regarding the Marxist-Leninist guerrillas. Unilateral information opportunities and, in many instances, ideological bias, combine to provide arguments that delegitimize established regimes and thus encourage guerrillas.

One of the major characteristics of the network is its international nature, which often assumes a global aspect. Not only are all the political and diplomatic resources of a superpower deployed, but the resources of the global hostility toward democracy and free enterprise are equally well harnessed. Soviet proxies throughout the world (Ethiopia, Vietnam, Eastern Europe, Angola, Mozambique, and South Yemen) and Soviet allies or circumstantial allies (Libya, Syria, or such genuinely nonaligned but consistently anticapitalist and antidemocratic regimes as Algeria, Iran, and Iraq) are all encouraged to become network members at a very low cost. They may even do so of their own volition, for reasons having infinitely more to do with anti-Americanism than with national interest.

To a large extent, Western governments and important parties or groups behave similarly for similar reasons, that is, anti-Americanism is the least costly and most spectacular way of underscoring national independence. This applies to Mexico and France but also to Latin American countries like Ecuador until recently and Argentina after the Falklands experience.

The global aspects of the network, particularly the role of radical and Marxist regimes in the Third World, play an essential role in transforming Central America and the Caribbean into a Soviet-oriented scene of struggle. Libya was the largest supplier of aid to the NJM regime in Grenada, and Iranian, Palestinian, and other radical Middle Eastern actors play a well-known and prominent role in training, financing, arming and politically supporting Central American Marxist-Leninists. These facts serve both to magnify Soviet ability to deny involvement in the region and to reduce Soviet costs for actual involvement. Central American Marxists are quite open in proclaiming their solidarity with anti-Western and, particularly, anti-American Third World actions, feelings, and policies. The effect is to paralyze the United States by forcing it to increase its spending of resources and political capital in the western hemisphere and to lower its commitments of resources for U.S. or Western involvement elsewhere in the Third World.

NOTES

1. H. Michael Erisman, "Colossus Challenged: U.S. Caribbean Policy in the 1980's," in H. Michael Erisman and John D. Martz, eds., *Colossus Challenged: The Struggle for Caribbean Influence* (Boulder, Colo.: Westview, 1982), p. 35. William M. LeoGrande went perhaps farther by writing that "Claims of an East-West confrontation distort reality in two ways—by making it sound as if the Salvadoran revolution is a Cuban creation, as if it is a purely military struggle" (William M. LeoGrande, "A Splendid Little War: Drawing the Line in El Salvador," in Stanford Central America Action Network, *Revolution in Central America* [Boulder, Colo.: Westview, 1983], p. 111). Viron Vaky, former assistant secretary of state for inter-American affairs under the Carter administration and one of the main actors in that administration's handling of the Nicaraguan civil war, considers that one of the major errors of the Reagan policy is that it "approaches Central America from the top, i.e., from the perspective of the cold war. Its policies and tactics are, in effect, designed for extra-regional ends, with an eye to Moscow and Havana, even though they have local content, impact, and cost" (Viron Vaky, "Reagan's Central American Policy: An Isthmus Restored," in Robert S. Leiken, ed., *Central America: Anatomy of Conflict* [New York: Pergamon, 1984], p. 252).

2. *The Americas at the Crossroads*, Report of the Inter-American Dialogue, Woodrow Wilson International Center for Scholars, Washington, D.C., April 1983, p. 41.

3. Even more explicit in this sense is Charles Maechling in "Insurgency and Counterinsurgency: The Role of Strategic Theory," *Parameters*, Autumn 1984, p. 40. Maechling states, "In areas like Latin America, where the tides of revolutionary change

are likely to run strongly for the next 50 years, the United States should try to navigate the current, not dam it up. A couple of tiny Yugoslavias south of the border would pose no security threat to the United States and would be far harder nuts for Moscow and Havana to penetrate than the present festering sores of poverty and injustice. The goal should be to prevent the domination of revolutionary change by Moscow and Havana, not to prevent such change from taking place."

4. Representatives Gerry E. Studds, Barbara Ann Mikulski, and Robert Edgar, "Who Makes Up the Opposition in El Salvadaor?" in Marvin E. Gettleman et al., eds., *El Salvador: Central America in the New Cold War* (New York: Grove Press, 1981), pp. 115–16.

5. Carlos Rangel, *The Latin Americans: Their Love-Hate Relationship with the United States* (New York: Harcourt Brace Jovanovich, 1977), p. 99.

6. Carlos Rangel, *L'Occident et le Tiers Monde* (Paris: Robert Laffont, 1982), p. 66.

7. Quoted in Gustavo Gutierrez, "The Church in the Process of Liberation," in Stanford Central America Action Network, *Revolution in Central America*, p. 369.

8. Moscow Domestic Television Service, March 3, 1983, in Foreign Broadcasting Information Service (FBIS), USSR Daily Report, March 4, 1983, p. K4.

9. FBIS, Daily Report, Latin America, April 3, 1981, p. P10.

10. Mario Menendez Rodriguez, *El Salvador: Una Auténtica Guerra Civil*, Educa, San Jose, Costa Rica, 1981, p. 143.

11. Menendez, quoting FPL leader "Camilo," in ibid., p. 70.

12. Ibid., p. 72.

13. Manifesto of the People's Revolutionary Movement, MRP-IXIM, Guatemala, December 1982, in FBIS, Daily Report, Latin America, December 28, 1982, p. P10. It is important to note that MRP-IXIM is a far-left group formed by extremists of the Guatemalan Marxist-Leninist groups, including ORPA, EGP, the Communist Party (PGT), and the Rebel Armed Forces (FAR). All are opposed to any political compromise, including the use of political fronts, as well as to the unification of the Guatemalan Marxist left.

14. Menendez, *El Salvador*, p. 143.

15. The text is published in *Contemporary Marxism*, no. 1 (Spring 1980): 89–99.

16. Ibid., p. 90.

17. Ibid.

18. Ibid.

19. Ibid.

20. MRP-IXIM, in FBIS, Daily Report, Latin America, December 28, 1982, p. P10.

21. EGP, in *Contemporary Marxism*, no. 1 (Spring 1980).

22. Ibid., p. 92.

23. *El Nuevo Diario*, Managua, Nicaragua, October 8, 1981, p. 8b.

24. Commander "Pedro," FBIS, Daily Report, Latin America, June 4, 1980, annex, p. 9.

25. Communiqué of ERP's General Command, in FBIS, March 15, 1983, p. P12.

26. *Maurice Bishop Speaks: The Grenada Revolution, 1979–1983* (New York: Pathfinder Press, 1983), p. 206.

Some Insights
Derived from the
Grenada Documents

Herbert Romerstein

During the French student disturbances of the late 1960s, one of the bits of graffiti found on the walls of Paris read, "I am a Marxist—of the Groucho tendency." Similarly, the sampling of Grenada documents released by the U.S. government prior to the opening of the entire archive puts one in mind of the 1934 Marx Brothers' movie *Duck Soup*, not Karl Marx's *Critique of the Gotha Programme*. Although the latter provided the concept of the "dictatorship of the proletariat," the New Jewel Movement's goal, in some ways it was Groucho Marx's mythical kingdom of Freedonia that the movement achieved. Perhaps Karl Marx described the phenomenon when he wrote in *The Eighteenth Brumaire of Louis Bonaparte* that "Hegel remarks somewhere that all facts and personages of great importance in world history occur, as it were, twice. He forgot to add: the first time as tragedy, the second as farce."

Marx "forgot to add" that the farce may contain a heavy dose of tragedy. This, indeed, is one of the lessons of the Grenada revolution. A small group of revolutionaries, taking control of a tiny island in the Caribbean, attached itself to a dictatorial world power and attempted to emulate that power and its satellites. Although, in the documents, many names of well-known people are misspelled and basic Marxist-Leninist slogans are misstated, Maurice Bishop's regime was bent on imposing a Soviet-style dictatorship.

On September 13, 1982, Bishop made a secret speech to a meeting of the members of his New Jewel Movement. He outlined what the movement had accomplished and what it intended to accomplish. The speech was entitled "Line of March for the Party." Each copy was stamped "Confidential" and was hand numbered. There is some indication that members had to return the copies after using them in special study classes.

The purpose of the party's "march," according to Bishop, was to "Ensure the leading role of the working class through its Marxist/Leninist Party backed by some form of the dictatorship of the proletariat." Bishop described the functioning of the dictatorship in these memorable words: "Just consider, comrades, how laws are made in this country. Laws are made in this country when Cabinet agrees and when I sign a document on behalf of Cabinet. And then that is what everybody in the country—like it or don't like it—has to follow. Or consider how people get detained in this country. We don't go and call for no votes. You get detained when I sign an order after discussing it with the National Security Committee of the Party or with a higher Party body. Once I sign it—like it or don't like it—it's up the hill for them."

This was not the image of the Grenadan revolution given to noncommunists. Bishop's speech revealed how the deception was carried out. He pointed out that after the 1979 revolution a ruling council was formed that included "the petty [*sic*]-bourgeoisie, the upper petty-bourgeoisie and the national bourgeoisie." Among those former council members he named were Lloyd Noel and Pam Buxo. Bishop reported that "Lloyd Noel is in detention, Pam Buxo is out of the country." According to Bishop, "there is absolutely no doubt that we have a hegemonic control on power and over all the capital areas of the State."

The deception was no accident. Bishop said, "this was done deliberately so that imperialism won't get too excited and would say 'well they have some nice fellas in that thing; everything alright.' And as a result wouldn't think about sending in troops. That was the mistake, for example, the comrades in Gambia made a few months ago. Remember the Gambia Coup E'tat [*sic*] a few months ago? What was the first thing those comrades did? They say 'we are Marxist-Leninists and we have just had a Marxist-Leninist Revolution and we go wipe out the bourgeoisie.' The same day they overthrow them—same day, they didn't even give them three days. So fortunately, NJM had a little more sense than that."[1]

The method adopted by Bishop had been successfully used in Cuba and Nicaragua. It was described by Blas Roca, general secretary of the Popular Socialist Party of Cuba (the pre-Castro Communist Party), in an article in *World Marxist Review* for November 1960. According to Roca, "At first the country experienced a kind of dual rule, with administrative functions exercised both by the revolutionary power, as represented by the rebel army and its recognised leader Fidel Castro, and the provisional government, which enjoyed formal authority. In this government the right-wing elements had the upper hand, and among them were such compromisers and saboteurs as President Urrutia, Foreign Minister Roberto Agramonte, Prime Minister Miro Cardona." This government of democratic Cubans did not last long, since the guns were in the hands of the "honest revolutionaries," as Roca referred to the leaders of the "rebel army." Roca boasted, "As the revolution progressed, the conciliators and saboteurs gradually left the government."[2] In Nicaragua, too, democratic personalities such as Mrs. Violeta Chamorro and Alfonso Robelo did not last long in the Sandinista junta.

The Bishop regime soon became part of the Soviet solar system. During a meeting on March 10, 1983, with Grenadan Army Chief of Staff Einstein Louison, N. V. Ogarkov, a Marshal of the Soviet Union and the Soviet Chief of Staff, explained the situation. According to the official Grenadan report of the meeting, "The Marshal said that over two decades ago, there was only Cuba in Latin America, today there are Nicaragua, Grenada and a serious battle going on in El Salvador. The Marshal of the Soviet Union then stressed that United States imperialism would try to prevent progress but that there were no prospects for imperialism to turn back history. Moreover, Marshal Ogarkov emphasised that in an aggressive climate the military people have tasks to do. He explained that since Grenada was located close to US imperialism and was not developed militarily the Grenada Revolution would have to be specifically vigilant at all times. Furthermore, the Marshal declared that once the masses have a burning desire for progress the leadership should move ahead decisively and firmly. On that point Marshal Ogarkov assured Major Louison that the plans outlined by Prime Minister Maurice Bishop during his visit to the Soviet Union in 1982 were good and had the support of the Grenadan people. Further still, the Marshal of the Soviet Union reminded Major Louison that the Soviet Union would contribute to raising the combat readiness and preparedness of the Armed Forces of Grenada."[3]

In a report to Bishop and the party leadership dated July 11, 1983, the Grenadan ambassador to the Soviet Union, W. Richard Jacobs, outlined Soviet thinking based on his meetings with officials of the International Department of the Communist Party of the Soviet Union (CPSU). The Soviets, according to Jacobs, looked on the New Jewel Movement as a Communist Party. He pointed out, however, that "by itself, Grenada's distance from the USSR, and its small size, would mean that we would figure in a very minute way in the USSR's global relationships. Our revolution has to be viewed as a world-wide process with its original roots in the Great October Revolution. For Grenada to assume a position of increasingly greater importance, we have to be seen as influencing at least regional events. We have to establish ourselves as the authority on events in at least the English-speaking Caribbean, and be the sponsor of revolutionary activity and progressive developments in this region at least. At the same time, we have to develop and maintain normal state to state relations with our neighbours and concretely operationalise our good-neighbourlyness policy. The twice per year meetings with the progressive and revolutionary parties in the region is therefore critical to the development of closer relations with the USSR. In order to keep both the Embassy and the Soviets informed of the outcome of such meetings, perhaps a good model would be for a member of the CC to pay a visit to the USSR after each such meeting. The mission of such a person could without difficulty be mixed with other activities. We must ensure though that we become the principal point of access to the USSR for all these groups even to the point of having our Embassy serve as their representative while in the USSR . . . Of all the regional possibilities, the most likely candidate for special attention is Surinam. If we can be an overwhelming influence on Surinam's international behaviour, then our importance in the Soviet scheme of thing will be greatly enhanced [*sic*]. To the extent that we can take credit for bringing any other country into the progressive fold, our prestige and influence would be greatly enhanced [*sic*]. Another candidate is Belize. I think that we need to do some work in that country."[4]

It took some time before the New Jewel Movement could look upon itself as a full-fledged Soviet surrogate. The Grenadans' relationship with the Soviets was aided by the Workers' Party of Jamaica (the official Communist Party of that island) whose leader, Trevor Monroe, wrote to Bishop on October 16, 1969, "How are things with you and the Soviets? Is there anything you want us to do?"[5]

According to an undated report by Jacobs, formal relations with the CPSU started in June 1980 with Bernard Coard's visit to the USSR, where he signed a party-to-party agreement. This agreement included a provision for sending Grenadan students to Soviet Communist Party training schools.[6] Two reports found in the files show that Grenadans were trained at the Lenin School, a Soviet institution that has existed since the 1920s to train foreign Communist cadres. Courses included such topics as: the historical experience of the CPSU, party organization, social psychology and propaganda, and the theory and tactics of the world revolutionary movement.[7]

Jacobs complained in his report that Grenada was handled by the section of the International Department that dealt with the English-speaking western hemisphere. He wrote, "We are faced with a situation therefore where Grenada has been put in a Department which contains only countries of capitalist orientation and the two big capitalist giants in our region." Another complaint was that when high-level Grenadans visited the Soviet Union, they were received by "relatively low level people," not by the top party leadership. The Cubans explained to the Grenadans that it took them fifteen years to achieve the top-level relationships that the Grenadans were seeking.[8] During an April 1983 visit to Moscow, however, Bishop met with Gromyko.

The Grenadans recognized that "Cuba is the leader of the Revolutionary Movement in this part of the world." In light of this, it is understandable that when Grenadan delegates went to international meetings they often stopped in Cuba to receive instructions. For example, the Grenadan delegate to a conference in Libya in June 1982 stopped in Cuba to meet with Manuel Pineiro, the head of the Americas Department of the Central Committee of the Communist Party of Cuba, the covert action arm of the Castro regime. Godwin Horsford, the Grenadan delegate, reported that Pineiro "explained to us the nature of the Conference and put forward key guidelines for our approach to the major issues of the meeting."[9]

Pineiro also played an important role in an operation against the Socialist International (S.I.). The New Jewel Movement and the Sandinistas of Nicaragua served as the "Trojan horse" for this operation. Among the documents found in the New Jewel Movement files was a report signed by Pineiro that describes the internal workings of the Socialist International.[10]

A "secret regional caucus" was established by some parties in the Socialist International in concert with the Nicaraguan Sandinista Party (which has observer status in the S.I.) and the Cuban Communist Party. Its aim was to plan the subversion of the International. A meeting of the "secret regional caucus" was held in Managua on January 6–7, 1983, chaired by Antonio Jarquin of the International Department of the FSLN (Sandinistas). In attendance were Chris DeRiggs of the New Jewel Movement, Grenada; Hector Oqueli, international affairs secretary of the National Revolutionary Movement (MNR) of El Salvador (the MNR, although a member party of the Socialist International, is affiliated with the political front of the Marxist-Leninist insurgent movement in El Salvador, the Revolutionary Democratic Front); Freda (no last name given) of the Radical Party of Chile; Paul Miller of the People's National Party (PNP) of Jamaica; and Silva (no first name given) of the Communist Party of Cuba.

In his report to the Political Bureau of the New Jewel Movement, Chris DeRiggs explained the agenda of the meeting, which included "Initiatives to be taken to strengthen the position of progressive forces of Latin America and the Caribbean within the organization. Initiatives to neutralize forces within S.I. that are against us." He pointed out that "our strongest allies in Europe are the Nordic S.I. parties and that of Holland. There is also good potential with the U.D.P. [sic, NDP, or New Democratic Party] of Canada. Our principal enemies are to be found among the parties of Scares and Horgo [sic, Longo] in Portugal and Italy respectively—the Social Democrats of the U.S.A. are also our sworn enemies." DeRiggs claimed that of the fourteen members of the S.I. committee for Latin America and the Caribbean, "there are seven parties that are generally progressive and some within Marxist-Lennist [sic] trend." He looked to three new parties in the S.I. to provide control of the committee to the "progressive forces." They were the Puerto Rican Independence Party, the Working People's Alliance of Guyana, and the Progressive Labour Party of St. Lucia.[11]

In his report on the November 1982 S.I. bureau meeting in Switzerland, DeRiggs recommended that S.I. parties in the region send delegations to

Western Europe to "help to exploit contradictions existing even within the Membership of S.I. Parties like the Socialist Party of Portugal."[12]

The New Jewel Movement knew little about the history and ideology of the Socialist International. But it knew that it was uncomfortable in a democratic movement. An NJM report, "Socialist International—An Assessment from Grenada's Perspective," gives ample evidence of the lack of both knowledge and comfort. It was written to re-evaluate NJM membership. The report starts thus: "Many claim for the Socialist International a history dating back to more than a century. It would appear that initially the name was the First International." The history of the International was known to the NJM only through the claims of many, not through standard writings on the subject. And, of course, the S.I. is the Second, not the First, International. The arguments for S.I. membership were that the NJM could obtain support for Grenada through the S.I. and could in turn provide support through the organization to "progressive struggles" in such places as southern Africa, the Western Sahara, Palestine, El Salvador, Nicaragua, and other parts of Latin America. The NJM was still troubled. The report said, "Some would argue yes, these are your objectives, yes, they are realized through membership in SI. But what about principles? The ideology of SI is Democratic Socialism."[13] The Grenadans opted to substitute expediency for principles and to remain in the S.I.

The value of the International to the Marxist-Leninists of the NJM was indicated in a report on the S.I.'s March 1981 emergency meeting on Latin America (which took place in Panama). Unison Whiteman, a high-ranking NJM and government official and the author of the report, described a resolution on El Salvador taken up by the meeting. Carlos Andres Perez of Venezuela "insisted on adding the names of Cuba and the Soviet Union to the resolution demanding an end to the supply of arms to El Salvador! . . . For hours he persisted. Sweden and Grenada spoke out forcefully on the issue. Grenada pointed out that the U.S. supply of arms to the junta is a notorious fact, that the U.S. officially and publicly stated this; that S.I. should not speculate on where the freedom fighters are getting arms from; that, in any event, we should not equate arms for the oppressors with weapons to defend the people in their just struggle. Finally, the El Salvador Comrades said they were prepared to accept a compromise formula that names no country but makes it clear that it is the U.S. that is being condemned. The house accepted this approach."[14]

According to Whiteman, the U.S. tactic was to accuse the Salvador insurgents of not truly wanting a negotiated settlement but preferring "the bloodshed." Whiteman continued, "As a means of defeating [the U.S. tactic], the Conference offered the services of S.I. Chairman, Willi Brandt as mediator in the conflict. This initiative ensures that the U.S. cannot propose someone favourable to their own interest. Brandt is sympathetic for the freedom fighters but the U.S. will have difficulty rejecting him for he is a Nobel Peace Prize Winner with stature world wide. This counter tactic would therefore give the comrades time to carry on the military and the political struggle together."[15] In this instance the New Jewel Movement helped provide political support to the Marxist-Leninist insurgents in El Salvador so that they could continue the bloodshed while pretending to want negotiations.

In addition to political training for Grenadans by the Soviet Union, Cuba, and other bloc countries, even more sinister training was in the works. A 1982 document on the letterhead of the Grenadan Embassy in Cuba reveals that the Vietnamese government had offered to train twenty Grenadans in such skills as "re-education of anti-social and counter-revolutionary elements."[16] A February 1982 letter from Hudson Austin, then general of the army, to Yuri Andropov, then head of the KGB, requested training for three "comrades" in counterintelligence and one "comrade" in intelligence. According to Austin, this request was based on a discussion that included Vladimir Klimentov ("then attached to the Soviet Embassy in Jamaica"), and Maurice Bishop, Liam James, and Austin. Austin continued, "We thank you once again for the tremendous assistance which our armed forces have received from your Party and Government in the past."[17]

The extent of the assistance Austin referred to has been indicated by the U.S. government's display of samples of the substantial weaponry provided by the Soviet bloc to tiny Grenada. The United States has also distributed copies of treaties in which the Soviet Union, Cuba, and other countries in the bloc agree to supply many more weapons than could possibly be needed for the defense of Grenada.

The entire Grenada archive has now been opened to scholars. The documents provide a valuable insight into the New Jewel Movement, its self-image, and its role in the Soviet program. Although small and remote, Grenada was of sufficient value for the Soviet Union to make available significant resources to train and equip Grenadan Marxist-Leninists for both violent and political struggle. The NJM regime in Grenada desired to help in carrying out the Soviet program for the western hemisphere.

The Cubans serve as the primary Soviet surrogate in the western hemisphere. The Grenadans could hope only to be a junior partner to the Cubans. The documents show that high-level Cubans acted to maximize the efforts of the New Jewel Movement. These efforts included aid to revolutionary groups in the Caribbean and subversion of such democratic international organizations as the Socialist International. Cuban advice, as well as assistance from other Soviet surrogates, aided the NJM in creating a "dictatorship of the proletariat" in Grenada.

Further analysis of the Grenada documents should provide valuable lessons to other countries threatened by Marxist-Leninist revolutionaries linked to the Soviet Union and Cuba.

NOTES

1. Document 1, "Line of March for the Party" (Presented by Comrade Maurice Bishop, Chairman, Central Committee, to general meeting of the party, Monday, September 13, 1982), in Michael Ledeen and Herbert Romerstein, eds., *Grenada Documents: An Overview and Selection* (Washington, D.C.: Department of State and Department of Defense, 1984).

2. Blas Roca, *World Marxist Review*, November 1960.

3. Document 24 (Report of meeting between Chiefs of General Staff of Soviet armed forces and People's Revolutionary Armed Forces of Grenada, March 10, 1983), in Ledeen and Romerstein, *Grenada Documents*.

4. Document 26, "Grenada's Relations with the USSR" (Report by W. Richard Jacobs, July 11, 1983), ibid.

5. Trevor Monroe to Maurice Bishop, October 16, 1969, on letterhead of Workers' Party of Jamaica, Grenada Documents, National Archives.

6. "Relations with the CPSU" (Report by W. Richard Jacobs, n.d.), Grenada Documents, National Archives.

7. Report to N.J.M. Organising Committee from Party Cell at CPSU International Leninist School, September 1–30, 1983, Grenada Documents, National Archives.

8. "Relations with the CPSU," Grenada Documents, National Archives.

9. Document 34 (Report on the General Congress of the World Center for the Resistance of Imperialism, Zionism, Racism and Reaction), in Ledeen and Romerstein, *Grenada Documents*.

10. Document 33 (Report on the Socialist International by Manuel Pineiro, n.d. but rubberstamped July 8, 1981), ibid.

11. Document 39 (Report on meeting of Secret Regional Caucus held in Managua, January 6–7, 1983), ibid.

12. Document 40 (Report on Socialist International Bureau Meeting, November 3–4, 1982, in Basel, Switzerland), ibid.

13. Document 38, "Socialist International—An Assessment from Grenada's Perspective," ibid.

14. Document 41 (Report on the Emergency S.I. in Panama, February 28 and March 1, 1981), ibid.

15. Ibid.

16. Document 18 (Note on letterhead of Grenadan Embassy in Cuba, dated February 1982, on discussions with Vietnamese ambassador to Cuba), ibid.

17. Document 27 (Draft letter, dated February 17, 1982, on letterhead of the Ministry of the Interior, from Hudson Austin to Yuri Andropov, head of KGB), ibid.

The Network:
Using Disinformation

H. Joachim Maitre

The Soviet Union and the other countries of the socialist community, all the forces of peace and progress the world over, side with the people of El Salvador in the struggle and strongly denounce the actions of the imperialists seeking to destabilize the situation and build up tensions in Central America.

V. Krestianinov, *International Affairs*, Moscow, July 1983

In every country, there is a sort of "big computer" that organizes the society. But in Russia, there is a computer that connects with other small computers in countries all over the world and converges in a powerful machine. This is just what the democracies do not have. Every one is independent and tries to protect itself, and there is no relation to the rest. That is why it is so much easier for the Communists. Those who want to fight against the right can count on the whole machinery of the left. On the contrary, those fighting against them have no network of communication.

Jose Napoleon Duarte, president of El Salvador,
Washington Times, June 6, 1985

We have been subjected in this country to a very sophisticated lobbying campaign by a totalitarian government . . . There has been a disinformation program that is virtually worldwide, and we know that the Soviets and Cubans have such a disinformation network that is beyond anything we can match.

Ronald Reagan, *El Salvador News-Gazette*, August 13, 1985

In the United States, the mere mention of international communism as the driving force behind "wars of national liberation" tends to provoke derision in so-called liberal circles. Violent communist takeovers in Laos, Cambodia, and Vietnam, in Angola, Mozambique, and Ethiopia—accomplished during the 1960s and 1970s—are attributed to local conflict or civil war rather than to the guiding fist of an international totalitarian movement. In spite of those instances, and the Cuban and Nicaraguan examples next door, liberal elites and their followers in the United States cling to their credo of liberation through revolution, generated by essentially indigenous forces.

The outstanding and undeniable fact about these "wars of national liberation," however, is that they have all enjoyed massive Soviet material and propaganda support, and that American liberals have consistently opposed United States intervention of any kind on the anticommunist side.

Communists have always come to power through violent takeovers—a tightly organized minority, assisted from the outside, seizes power over an unorganized and unwitting majority. Such takeovers always entail the use of "popular fronts" (consisting of communist and noncommunist elements), camouflage of the Communist Party's aim, and propaganda and disinformation designed to manipulate the international news media and foreign political decisionmakers.

All communist regimes invest heavily in propaganda and disinformation. Their principal goal is to disseminate false information about the nature of their political systems. When still consolidating power, the principal aim of their disinformation is to persuade others, particularly those abroad, that they are not really communists.

Such disinformation strategy has been strictly followed by the Sandinistas in Nicaragua. The history of the Sandinista movement, from its birth in the revolutionary underground in 1961 through its military victory in 1979 and including Managua today, is the story of a small vanguard of dedicated Marxist-Leninist professionals invoking the tactics and strategy of deception with the sole aim of camouflaging their movement's true identity. The Sandinistas' success in convincing thousands of American liberals that Sandinista power is rooted in nationalism, social democracy, and Christianity—rather than in Marxism-Leninism as "the scientific doctrine of the revolution"—is a towering monument to the powers of deception, a monument only slightly stained by the fingerprints of those who wanted to be deceived.

No account of the Sandinistas' ascension to power can be written without a chapter dedicated to their international support columns in the democracies. This consists of an army of hard-core professional revolutionaries and "well-meaning" idealists, of seasoned theorists of global revolution in Washington's Institute for Policy Studies or in the Council on Hemispheric Affairs, and of Sandinista followers united in such groups as the Coalition for a New Foreign and Military Policy, the Lawyers' Committee for International Human Rights, or various factions under the roof of Congress (see Appendix A).

THE NETWORK

Whatever may divide the professionals from the "useful idiots" (Lenin) in the ranks, the Network (as I shall call it) is held together by the membership's benign view and benevolent acts toward left-wing "revolutionary" movements. When a government under siege attempts to fight the revolutionaries, the Network protests the government's "violation of human rights" and asks Washington to withdraw all aid. When the revolutionaries gain power and announce that they are now communists, the Network cautions Washington against taking hard measures, for hard measures might drive the new regime into Moscow's arms. To the Network, the new communist regime is now "a reality," and "we must learn to live with it."

With its stereotypical predictability, the Network performs a valuable public relations and propaganda function for international communism. With its continuous activism against Washington's policies and aid programs designed to support fledgling democracies in their campaigns against armed and antidemocratic insurgencies, the Network systematically undermines, politically and ideologically, international communism's main target—the United States of America. The fight for El Salvador is a case in point.

In late May of 1985, while Jose Napoleon Duarte was visiting the United States and Congress was in the final phase of debating economic and military aid for El Salvador, the left's Network—thanks to the editorial policy of the *New York Times*—scored yet another subtle victory for disinformation on El Salvador. On May 23, 1985, the paper printed an op-ed piece authored by one Terry Karl, which misrepresented the strategic situation in El Salvador as a "military stalemate" and "an opportunity for a political compromise," and suggested that the United States Congress, "which holds the strings on the purse that maintains the Salvadoran military and economy," tip the alleged military balance in favor of a political settlement. "Congress should cut military aid," Karl wrote, in view of rebel leader Joaquin Villalobos's willingness to agree to a cease-fire—provided the United States "ended its aid to the Salvadoran military." Citing "positive, though fragile, signs for limited accommodation" in El Salvador, "undercut by attempts by the United States to escalate the war," Karl then pointed an accusing finger at the White House: "In the past year, the Reagan administration has deepened and transformed the nature of its military activity through support of aerial bombardment in the countryside, daily reconnaissance flights, the introduction of AC-47 gunships and an expanded helicopter fleet, increased training of the army and the direct involvement of American personnel in combat-related activities."[1]

When the *New York Times* published Karl's claim of a "military stalemate" in El Salvador and his request, based on such a "military stalemate," that Congress cut military aid to the Duarte government, the prestigious daily indirectly contradicted a professional analysis written by its Central American correspondent and printed in the *New York Times* just four days prior to the op-ed piece:

> After a five-year war that produced striking military and political gains, El Salvador's leftist guerrillas seem to have stumbled. Popular backing for the estimated 5000 armed guerrillas no longer seems to be growing and improved army tactics have forced them onto the defensive. Guerrilla commanders who once vowed to seize power in a few years now speak of a decades-long war of attrition. Rebel units that formerly sought out and defeated army battalions are now avoiding contact and concentrating on sabotage and political intimidation.[2]

Thus, contrary to the Network's Mr. Karl, there was no military stalemate in El Salvador in May 1985. The war, in fact, had been winding down throughout 1984 and early 1985. After more than five years of armed insurrection, the rebel forces of the Frente Farabundo Marti para la Liberación Nacional (FMLN) and the Frente Democrático Revolucionario (FDR) were farther from victory than ever before. El Salvador's armed forces were better equipped, more efficient, more professional, better led, and better motivated after a crash program of U.S. training. The war was thus fading, with the insurgents regressing from open warfare to small-scale harassment, terrorist-style assassinations and kidnappings, and destruction of economic targets.

The insurgents' military strategy had amounted to a war of attrition against the Salvadoran economy, the political structures, and the armed forces. The strategy's minimal objective had been to increase—within the context of a prolonged military stalemate—the political, economic, and military costs of the war to an intolerable degree and thus to force the government into negotiations, resulting in the rebels' victory through "power-sharing."

By May 1985, however, the insurgents had failed decisively on the political as well as the military front. Yet, although in early 1981 the word "negotiations" could not be found in the dictionary of insurgents seeking total victory, by early 1985 they had a degree of hope for gaining power through the back-door. "When you speak of negotiations, you speak of power-sharing," the FDR's spokesman Ruben Zamora confessed in October of 1984, admitting that "we thought before that total triumph was possible, but we have come to terms with reality."[3]

The new reality in El Salvador, however, included the political correlation of constitutional forces, with a solid majority in the National Assembly adamantly opposed to any deal with the insurgents and with the armed forces—mirabile dictu—guarding the constitution. President Duarte stated on June 1, 1984, with well-justified pride: "Our army has grown considerably, has received better training, and is imbued with a deep patriotic sentiment to defend the country and prevent our fall into the hands of Marxist subversives that try to implant a totalitarian dictatorship in El Salvador."[4]

The insurgents' "revolutionary campaigns" since 1979—when the Sandinistas triumphed in neighboring Nicaragua and a similar victory for El Salvador's Marxists seemed possible or even likely—have been marked by a chain of severe miscalculations. The key to those miscalculations is that, contrary to the picture painted by the American and international left-wing media, the Salvadoran insurgency at no time could rely on popular support. At the height of their military offensive in 1983, Archbishop Arturo Rivas y Damas summed up the insurgents' central failure: "If the Salvadoran guerrillas had popular support, they would have won by now."[5]

All wars of insurgency are long and slogging conflicts, often inconclusive. Such wars do not end suddenly, with one side declaring "victory." Insurgencies can simply fade away and then reappear when new strategic realities promise greater success.

Such is now the case with El Salvador's insurgency. The five factions that make up the FMLN cannot hope to win power by military means. Similarly, a "political solution" (that is, "power-sharing") is remote in light of the armed forces' strength and the insurgents' demonstrated weakness in the field. The insurgents' sole present hope rests elsewhere—namely, with the media and political forces in the United States that still favor and stubbornly advocate or demand a "political solution" for El Salvador, notwithstanding the changed strategic realities in the region.

These new realities, centered on the second Reagan presidency, run counter to an accommodation with Marxist-Leninist forces anywhere in Central America. El Salvador has been defined repeatedly by President Reagan as the main battlefield between democracy and communism in the western hemisphere, and El Salvador's success in combating its insurgency could not have been achieved without determined assistance from the United States. The defeat of the FMLN is the direct outcome of the U.S. Congress's commitment, signed into law in 1962 by President John F. Kennedy: "To prevent by whatever means may be necessary, including the use of arms, the Marxist-Leninist regime in Cuba from extending, by force or by threat of force, its aggressive or subversive activities to any part of the hemisphere."

Since Castro's advent to power in Cuba in 1959, the western hemisphere has been subjected to probing attacks by the Soviet Union and Cuba through surrogate force. This strategy reached an apex in 1979 with the Sandinista capture of Nicaragua. It has since been rolled back in 1983 in Grenada, and in 1984 in El Salvador.

The international left proclaimed publicly in 1982 that "the defence of Cuba, the protection and deepening of the gains made in Nicaragua, and the expansion of the newly unified guerrilla movement in Guatemala have all become part of a single movement that depends vitally upon a popular victory in El Salvador."6 With the vision of such "popular victory" turned into an illusion in El Salvador, the "single movement," through its propaganda and disinformation agencies, consequently resorts to its proven game of deception. Inventing its own realities, it denies that it has lost in El Salvador.

Terry Karl, author of the op-ed piece "Stanching Salvador Blood," was identified by the *New York Times* as a "visiting professor of political science at the University of California" and "a member of a delegation to El Salvador sponsored by the Washington-based Commission on U.S.–Central American Relations, a public-policy organization."7 But on previous op-ed pages, the *New York Times* had identified this very group as "a private advocacy organization."8 Advocating what?

The private Commission on U.S.–Central American Relations is, in fact, much more than a "private advocacy organization." It is, according to the Heritage Foundation's report on *The Left's Latin American Lobby* (1984), one of six major organizations in the United States whose fundamental ideological perspective is openly hostile to present U.S. policy in the hemisphere and openly supportive of existing and emerging "revolutionary" movements. The other five are the North American Congress on Latin America (NACLA), the Council on Hemispheric Affairs (COHA), the Washington Office on Latin America (WOLA), the Central America Historical Institute (CAHI), and the openly pro-Marxist Committee in Solidarity with the People of El Salvador (CISPES)—the People of El Salvador being, of course, the guerrillas.9 Among the hundreds of leftist and anarchist pressure groups opposed to the administration's Central American policy and friendly toward totalitarian movements, "this handful stands out as the largest, best organized and singularly most effective. In an area littered with amateurs, these are the professionals."10

Several individuals from these groups regularly generate opinion pieces for major newspapers in the United States and abroad. Their op-ed pieces can be found frequently in the *Washington Post* and the *New York Times* and are picked up by many of the 1,700 smaller dailies across the United States. Rarely is their political identity revealed—nor is their mission, which is to shade, embroider, and distort the truth. They have found company with several nationally syndicated columnists and have helped nurture an entire new generation of "journalists" who make it their duty to transform America's sworn enemies, such as Castro and Ortega, into misunderstood innocents, while at the same time portraying elected officials in Washington as the foes of freedom and democracy.

Anthony Lewis, the *New York Times'* star columnist, still denies that Marxists in power or fighting for power in Central America pose a threat to U.S. national security—accusing the Reagan administration of "paranoia."11

Meanwhile, the Network through its op-ed pieces and letters to the editor continues to distort Central American realities with the sole aim of deceiving the American public. In the three years between January 1981, when the FMLN guerrillas saw their "final offensive" fail, and December 1983, when a few guerrilla victories in the field convinced "military analysts" at *Newsweek* that "if the rebels are not likely to triumph immediately, they do seem to have time and momentum on their side,"[12] the American public was exposed to a continuous flood of falsified assessments of both military and political developments in El Salvador. News reports from the war-torn country, combined with evaluations issued by "liberal" think tanks in Washington, seemed to justify Americans' conclusion that "the war is going badly in El Salvador."[13]

Incompetent fieldwork by American journalists in El Salvador facilitated the growth of the left's disinformation network in the United States. The war was portrayed as a "civil war," fought without outside assistance by "the people" against a "repressive government" riddled with corruption. Denying the leading role of prominent urban Salvadoran Marxists within the FMLN—such as Shafik Handal, secretary-general of the Communist Party—the *New York Times*' own Raymond Bonner, a militant sympathizer with the revolt, reported "a homegrown, predominantly peasant revolution."[14] The notorious Commission on U.S.–Central American Relations originated a disinformation classic that was printed in the *New York Times* in 1983 and directed its falsehoods toward an American public still traumatized by U.S. involvement in Vietnam. The item stated that (1) the Salvadoran guerrillas did not threaten U.S. national security; (2) the Salvadoran government could not win the war; and (3) President Reagan would have to reintroduce the draft and "send United States ground troops to fight in El Salvador."[15]

In November 1983, the guerrilla movement's spokesman, Ruben Zamora, had announced "that an American intervention in Central America will come first in El Salvador . . . and that it will come fairly soon." Describing the military situation as critical for the government, because "the Salvadoran Army seems to have lost its will to fight," Zamora then outlined the FMLN's blueprint for its war of resistance against U.S. troops: "[we intend] to inflict maximum casualties on the invader. Then we will wait until the American public tires of seeing its young men coming home in plastic bags, and forces the withdrawal of the troops."[16]

In January 1984, Congressman James M. Shannon (a Massachusetts Democrat), as always the standard-bearer for "revolutionaries" in Central America, made public his fears of a "full-scale invasion" by the United States. Shannon's recipe for "long-term peace and stability" in El Salvador was negotiations between the rebels and the government, to be initiated through U.S. pressure on the Duarte government: "I believe that military assistance to the brutal government of El Salvador . . . should be ended now."[17] A "full-scale invasion" of El

Salvador had not, of course, been planned by the Reagan administration, and only through the twisting of reality could Americans be made to believe that cutting off military aid to El Salvador's armed forces would eventually result in "long-term peace and stability."

The fruits of systematic and concerted distortion of events in El Salvador became dramatically visible after a Gallup poll conducted in the spring of 1984: the American public, by a margin of 49 percent to 39 percent, opposed providing military assistance to governments in Central America, believing the United States should not get involved in the "internal affairs" of these nations. Although only one-fifth of those polled claimed to have followed developments in Central America "very closely," 72 percent expressed the "feeling" that U.S. involvement there could turn into a situation such as Vietnam and that the United States could (but should not) become more and more deeply involved.[18]

The Network's call for a cut-off of military aid to San Salvador, taken up by unsuspecting Americans, is central to the Network's strategy for the defeat of yet another U.S. ally and triumph of another "revolution." It should be remembered that in almost all cases since World War II where communist armed movements have fought their way to power, their victories were made possible by an American decision to reduce or eliminate the support previously granted to the incumbent regime. In the western hemisphere, the rise to power by Fidel Castro in Cuba and by the Sandinistas in Nicaragua was at least accelerated by the sudden denial of U.S. military aid to Batista and Somoza, respectively.

The Network's campaign against U.S. military aid for the government of El Salvador centers on that government's alleged inability or unwillingness to control its military and police forces. The "killing of innocent civilians" by the armed forces of a U.S. ally will not be tolerated by American citizens. Nor will the "systematic murder of the political opposition" through "civilian death squads operating under the eyes of the government." So abhorrent are such alleged practices that even certified nonmembers of the Network engage in collective indignation coupled with threats of a therapeutic cutoff of aid. Without offering a shred of evidence for his charges, William Griffith states: "Communists and other leftists have carried out some of these murders . . . but the vast majority of deaths are attributed to right-wing groups operating with the tolerance, if not guidance, of high-ranking Salvadoran army officers. And the government of El Salvador has done virtually nothing to bring the killers to justice . . . If the Salvadoran high command does little or nothing about the death squads, we should withhold a portion of our assistance."[19]

According to Carlos Marighella, a Marxist-Leninist theorist and accomplished Brazilian terrorist, "all revolutionary forces" operating against "repressive regimes" must transform "the political situation in the country into a military situation in which the militarists appear more and more to be the ones responsible for terror and violence, while the problems and lives of the people become truly catastrophic."[20]

"Appear to be"—the recipe for victory through deception in the target country, the United States of America, worked in the cases of South Vietnam and Nicaragua. It came close to success in El Salvador:

> By the most conservative account . . . more than 30,000 unarmed noncombatant civilians have been killed in four years of civil war in El Salvador, the vast majority of them by Salvadoran Government troops and security men. . . . The regime that Washington is propping up in El Salvador is riddled with corruption that staggers the imagination.
>
> Adam Hochschild, *New York Times*, December 22, 1983

> In El Salvador, where army-controlled murder of civilians has actually been rising (averaging more than 120 per week at the end of last year). . .
>
> John B. Oakes, *New York Times*, January 28, 1984

> At the heart, El Salvador's tragedy is that the civilian government itself is only a veneer pasted on the real source of power: the military and security forces.
>
> Editorial, *Boston Globe*, March 24, 1984

Caught in clichés, their perception paralyzed by prejudice about "right-wing death squads" and "government corruption," these partisan journalists were oblivious to the mounting terrorism of the revolutionaries. One remarkable feature of the election campaign in El Salvador in early 1984 was that assassins killed five of the sixty members of the constituent assembly. All of the five assassinated assemblymen had been members of the right-of-center coalition. In San Vicente, guerrillas killed two Red Cross ambulance drivers and blew up a schoolteacher with a hand grenade. In an attack on a passenger train in Chalatenango, guerrillas killed ten civilians, including several children. Ignoring these atrocities committed by its ideological ally, the Network continued its attacks on government forces.

"What would you do to stop the military advance of communist forces in the region?" Senator Paul E. Tsongas (a Massachusetts Democrat) was asked on CBS. His reply: "If you assume that Marxism is a reactive philosophy . . . then you have to move against the military in terms of taking away the appeal the guerrillas have."[21]

In March of 1984, Senator Tsongas and Congressman Shannon helped to bring the Network's defamation campaign against the Salvadoran military and police into America's living rooms. El Salvador's consul general in New Orleans, Roberto Santivanez, his head under wraps and name undisclosed, "testified" before Walter Cronkite (CBS) against Colonel Caranza, chief of the treasury police, and former defense minister Garcia. His "testimony" deflated and diplomatic assignment voided, Santivanez was then found to have been a hired witness. Promised $50,000, his appearance on CBS had been arranged by Robert S. White, former U.S. ambassador to El Salvador, who was fired by President Reagan in January 1981. White now heads a Center for Development Policy in Washington, one of several leftist "research organizations" founded and operating under the umbrella of the Institute for Policy Studies (IPS), well known for its work in international radical causes.

The role of the IPS and its numerous branches in the Network requires little elaboration.[22] It is a key role. Rael Jean Isaac has described IPS as "an enormous intelligence operation practicing both covert action and subversion" and suggests that "the activities of the Institute inevitably raise serious questions of motivation. IPS has consistently advocated policies that accord with the Soviet line . . . support for Soviet-linked revolutionary groups, apologetics for Soviet expansion, etc." Brian Crozier, director of the London Institute for the Study of Conflict, sees IPS as a "perfect intellectual front for Soviet activities which would be resisted if they were to originate openly from the KGB."[23]

Given the Institute's open operations, its wider political nature is well known in Washington. But the implications of the Institute's politics are apparently unclear to the media. Not just in the judgment of Rael Jean Isaac is "the most disturbing indication of IPS's increased legitimacy among opinion-makers as well as policy-makers . . . that IPS has practically become an institutional columnist for the *New York Times*." Isaac stresses that "IPS Fellows use their *Times* space to undermine support for every U.S. ally in the Third World and to glorify terrorist groups and countries that have gone over to the Soviet Bloc, while blaming untoward Soviet actions on American provocation."[24]

The Network's activism against the Reagan administration's policy for a Central America free of Soviet and Cuban rule cannot be evaluated without a thorough appreciation of the function the IPS occupies in the movement. From Washington and Amsterdam—through its international arm, the Transnational Institute—IPS coordinates and orchestrates campaigns and longer-range programs designed to achieve "socialism all over the world and not through peaceful revolution."[25]

But intellectual subversion of democratic systems can originate from sources other than IPS or CISPES (see Appendix B). There is the professor of international relations at Princeton who teaches (and writes in the *New York Times*) that "it is by no means self-evident that Soviet bases in Central America would seriously threaten the security of the United States."[26] There is the "expertise" of Charles Maechling, Jr., a former member of the National Security Council under presidents Kennedy and Johnson, who advises that "a couple of tiny Yugoslavias south of the border would pose no security threat to the United States."[27] And the nation hears from four-star general Wallace H. Nutting that "we have learned to live with Cuba for 25 years . . . we are going to have to learn to live with Nicaragua."[28]

The phenomenon of threat-denial, increasing among the nation's noncommunistic elites, must be seen as a more serious threat to U.S. national security than the activities of left-wing think tanks openly pursuing their political agenda. No one at IPS or CISPES would claim that the success of violent revolution in El Salvador would result in a "tiny Yugoslavia" (see Appendix C).

Preparation of vulnerability is the paramount object of Soviet covert and overt action in the United States. Its success in infiltrating the nation's intellectual texture must be seen as the most dramatic signal of the perils ahead. The orchestration of disinformation has made deeper inroads than ever thought possible.

APPENDIX A

Members of the Coalition for a New Foreign and Military Policy include:

American Friends Service Committee
Americans for Democratic Action
Center for International Policy
Center of Concern
Church Women United
Clergy and Laity Concerned
Council on Hemispheric Affairs
Democratic Socialists of America
Episcopal Peace Fellowship
Friends of the Earth
Friends of the Filipino People
Movement for a Free Philippines
National Assembly of Religious Women
National Council of Churches
National Gray Panthers
NETWORK
OXFAM America
Presbyterian Church (USA), Washington Office
SANE
Unitarian Universalist Association

United Methodist Church
War Resisters League
Washington Office on Latin America
Women's International League for Peace and Freedom
Women Strike for Peace
World Federalist Association
World Peace Makers

APPENDIX B

Fiction and Facts Regarding the Committee in Solidarity with the People of El Salvador (CISPES)

Fiction: CISPES supports democracy in El Salvador.

Fact: The 1982, 1984, and 1985 elections in El Salvador were denounced by CISPES. In line with the FMLN/FDR platform, CISPES does not advocate elections, demanding a "political solution."

Fiction: CISPES is dedicated to peaceful change in El Salvador.

Fact: CISPES actually promotes violence. Speakers at CISPES rallies have included Rafael Cancel Miranda of the Puerto Rico "Independence" movement FALN, representatives of the PLO, and various Marxist "revolutionary" groups.

Fiction: CISPES is nothing more than a group of citizens joined together to influence our government's policies.

Fact: CISPES is a well-organized active measures operation, intended to mobilize support in the U.S. for the guerrillas, set up with the help of Cuban intelligence officers operating under U.N. cover in New York.

Fiction: The objective of CISPES is to stop the U.S. from getting embroiled in another Vietnam-style war.

Fact: CISPES is committed to supporting the FMLN/FDR guerrillas. CISPES support for and contact with the FMLN/FDR was intended to "build an organization" designed to serve as a propaganda arm for the guerrillas in the United States.

Fiction: CISPES does not support communism in Central America.

Fact: The FMLN is named after an early leader of the Communist Party of El Salvador, Augustin Farabundo Marti, who served as an agent for Stalin's Comintern (Communist International) in the 1920s and early 1930s. FMLN leaders include several members of Marxist-Leninist groups, including Shafik Handal, secretary-general of the Communist Party of El Salvador.

FMLN/FDR Platform, January 1981 (El Salvador)

The Democratic Revolutionary Government, Its Composition and Platform of Political, Structural, and Social Change

The Democratic Revolutionary Government will be made up of represen- tatives from the popular and revolutionary movements and those democratic parties, organizations, sectors, and individuals who are disposed to participate in the carrying out of the present programme platform. This government will stand on a broad social and political base formed primarily by the working class, peasantry, and advanced middle sectors; closely tied to these will be all the social strata agreeing to carry out this platform: small and medium industrial businesspeople, merchants, artisans, small farmers. It will also include those honest professionals, progressive clergy, democratic parties like the National Revolutionary Movement, advanced sectors of the Christian Democrats, and worthy and honest officers of the army who will agree to serve the interest of the people; and all other sectors, groups, and individuals who will abide by a true democracy for the people, independent development, and popular liberation.

All these forces are presently becoming integrated into a democratic and revolutionary alliance in which the political and religious ideologies of each one are represented. The organic form of this revolutionary alliance in the service of the Salvadorean people will be a result of the consensus of all those who make it up.

Immediate Political Measures

1. The end of repression against the people in all its forms, and freedom for political prisoners.

2. Clarification of the whereabouts of all prisoners and disappeared per- sons since 1972 and punishment of those responsible (civilian or military) for crimes against the people.

3. Disarmament and dissolution of the repressive forces: ANSESAL (secret police), ORDEN (rural paramilitary police force), National Police, Hacienda Police, Customs Police, and their respective "Special Sections"; of the Gotera "Counter-Insurgency School" and the so-called "Armed Forces Engineering Instruction Center" in Zacatecoluca; of military patrols in the countryside and

suburbs; of the oligarchy's private paramilitary bands and of all type of organizations, real or nominal, dedicated to criminal actions against the people and their organizations. The misnamed Security Corps will be replaced by a civilian police force.

4. Dissolution of the actual powers of the state (executive, legislative, and judicial), repeal of the constitution and all decrees that have modified it or substituted for it. The Democratic Revolutionary Government will write a constitutive law and will organize the state and its activities with the aim of guaranteeing the rights and liberties of the people and the achievements of the goals and objectives of the revolution. In this respect, the Democratic Revolutionary Government will adhere to the "Universal Declaration of Human Rights" of the United Nations. The aforementioned constitutive law will be in effect while the Salvadorean people are creating a new constitution that faithfully reflects their interests.

5. The municipal structure of power will become an organ of full participation by the people in the running of the state, a true organ of the new power of the people.

6. The Democratic Revolutionary Government will carry out an intense program of liberating education, culture, and organization among the broad masses of the people in order to promote their conscious incorporation into the development, strengthening, and defense of the revolutionary process.

7. Strengthen and develop the Popular Army, which will be joined by those troops, sub-officers and officers of the present army who maintain a clean conduct, repel foreign intervention in the revolutionary process, and support the liberation struggle of our people. The new army will be the true armed wing of the people, will be at their service, will be absolutely loyal to their interests and their revolution; will be an armed forces that truly and patriotically defends our sovereignty and self-determination and is a decided supporter of peaceful coexistence among peoples.

8. Our country will be withdrawn from CONDECA (Central American Defense Council), TIAR, and any other military or police organism that is an instrument of intervention.

9. The Democratic Revolutionary Government will establish diplomatic and commercial relations with other countries, without discriminating because of different social systems, but based on equality of rights, coexistence, and respect for self-determination. Special attention will be paid to the development of friendly relations with the other Central American countries (including Panama and Belize), to uphold peace and the principle of nonintervention. In particular, fraternal relations with Nicaragua will be cultivated, as an expression of a community of ideals and interests between our revolution and the Sandinista revolution. Our country will join the movement of nonaligned states

and will develop policies invariably affiliated with the defense of world peace and in favor of détente.

Structural Changes

The Democratic Revolutionary Government will proceed to:

1. Nationalize the entire banking and financial system. This measure will not affect the deposits and other interests of the public.

2. Nationalize foreign commerce.

3. Nationalize the industries, now in private hands, which produce and distribute electricity.

4. Nationalize the petroleum refineries.

5. Expropriate, conformant with national interest, monopolized business in industry, commerce, and the services.

6. Carry out a deep agrarian reform that will put the land, now in the hands of the large landholders, at the disposal of the great masses of the people who work it, conformant with an effective plan that will benefit the great majority of poor and middle peasants and agricultural salaried workers, and which will promote the development of agriculture and livestock. The agrarian reform will not affect the small and medium landowners, who will receive support and economic stimulus to improve their production.

7. Carry out an urban reform that will benefit the great majority, without affecting the small and medium proprietors.

8. Fundamentally transform the tax system, so that the burden of taxes will not fall on the workers. Indirect taxes on articles and services of general consumption will be reduced. This will be possible not only through a reform of the tax system, but also because the state will receive a large income from its activities in the nationalized sector of the economy.

9. Establish effective mechanisms of credit and technical and economic loans for small and medium private enterprises in all branches of the economy.

10. Establish an effective planning system for the national economy that will permit balanced development.

Social Measures

The Democratic Revolutionary Government will orient its work in the social sphere toward the following achievements:

1. Create enough jobs to absorb unemployment in the shortest possible time.

2. Effect a just salary policy based on:

    (a) regulation of salaries, taking into account the cost of living;

(b) an energetic policy of control and reduction of the prices of necessary articles and services; and
(c) a substantial increase in social services for the masses of the people
(Social Security, education, recreation, health, and so on).
3. Undertake a massive plan to construct housing for the people.
4. Create a national health system, which will guarantee efficient medical
service, primarily preventative, to the entire population (urban and rural).
5. Carry out a massive literacy campaign that will eliminate the social
blemish of illiteracy in the shortest possible time.
6. Develop a national education system that will ensure primary education
for the entire population of school age and will substantially broaden secondary
and university education, raising the quality and diversity of scientific and
technical education at all levels and progressively eliminating its costs to the
people.
7. Promotion and dissemination of cultural activity on a large scale,
effectively stimulating and supporting national artists and writers, reviving and
developing the cultural heritage of the nation, incorporating the best of universal culture into that of the people, and organizing access by the people in all
manifestations of culture.

NOTES

1. Terry Karl, "Stanching Salvador Blood," *New York Times*, May 23, 1985.

2. James LeMoyne, "Salvador Puts Guerrillas on the Defensive," *New York Times*,
May 19, 1985.

3. Clifford Krauss, "Leftists Lose Optimism About Soon Prevailing in Central America," *Wall Street Journal*, October 15, 1984.

4. Inaugural speech, San Salvador, June 1, 1984.

5. Quoted in *La Nación Internacional* (Costa Rica), September 22, 1983.

6. James Dunkerley, *The Long War: Dictatorship and Revolution in El Salvador*
(London: Junction Books, 1982), p. 163.

7. Karl, "Stanching Salvador Blood."

8. Adam Hochschild, "Backing Salvador 'Insanity,'" *New York Times*, December 22,
1983.

9. "The Committee in Solidarity with the People of El Salvador seeks to educate and
mobilize public opinion against U.S. intervention in El Salvador and Central America
and in solidarity with the FMLN-FDR, the legitimate representative of the Salvadoran
people" (*Alert!* [Official CISPES monthly], April 1985).

10. John Holmes and Bill Outlaw, "The Network. Target: Reagan's Central American
Policy," *Washington Times*, April 9, 1985.

11. Anthony Lewis, "Method in the Madness?" *New York Times*, April 7, 1985.

12. *Newsweek*, December 12, 1983.

13. Editorial, *Boston Globe*, March 3, 1984.

14. Raymond Bonner, *Weakness and Deceit* (New York: Times Books, 1984), p. 111.

15. Hochschild, "Backing Salvador 'Insanity.'"

16. Stephen Kinzer, "Rebel in El Salvador Predicts U.S. Intervention There in '84," *New York Times*, November 12, 1983.

17. James Shannon in a Dear Friend letter, House of Representatives, Washington, D.C., January 13, 1984.

18. *Boston Globe*, June 10, 1984.

19. William Griffith, "El Salvador's Death Squads Must Go," *Reader's Digest*, April 1984.

20. Quoted in *The Report of the President's National Bipartisan Commission on Central America* (New York: Macmillan, 1984), p. 104.

21. On CBS with Walter Cronkite, May 9, 1984.

22. See Rael Jean Isaac and Eric Isaac, *The Coercive Utopians* (Chicago: Regnery Gateway, 1983); and Allan C. Brownfeld and J. Michael Waller, *The Revolution Lobby* (Washington, D.C.: Council for Inter-American Security/Inter-American Security Educational Institute, 1985).

23. Rael Jean Isaac, *America the Enemy: Profile of a Revolutionary Think Tank* (Washington: Ethics and Public Policy Center, 1980), p. 15.

24. Ibid.

25. Ibid., p. 16.

26. Richard H. Ullman, "Plain Talk on Central America," *New York Times*, July 10, 1983.

27. Charles Maechling, Jr., "Insurgency and Counterinsurgency," *Parameters* 14, no. 3.

28. *New York Times*, June 30, 1985.

Index